The 100 Commandments
of a
Black Queen

The 100 Commandments of a
Black Queen

Affirmations for the Soul

Livvy Liv

LIV
ONE CO.
Liv, Learn, Create

To my beautiful mother, a real Black Queen.
I love you

-Livvy Liv

Royal Count

I	=1
V	=5
X	=10
L	=50
C	=100

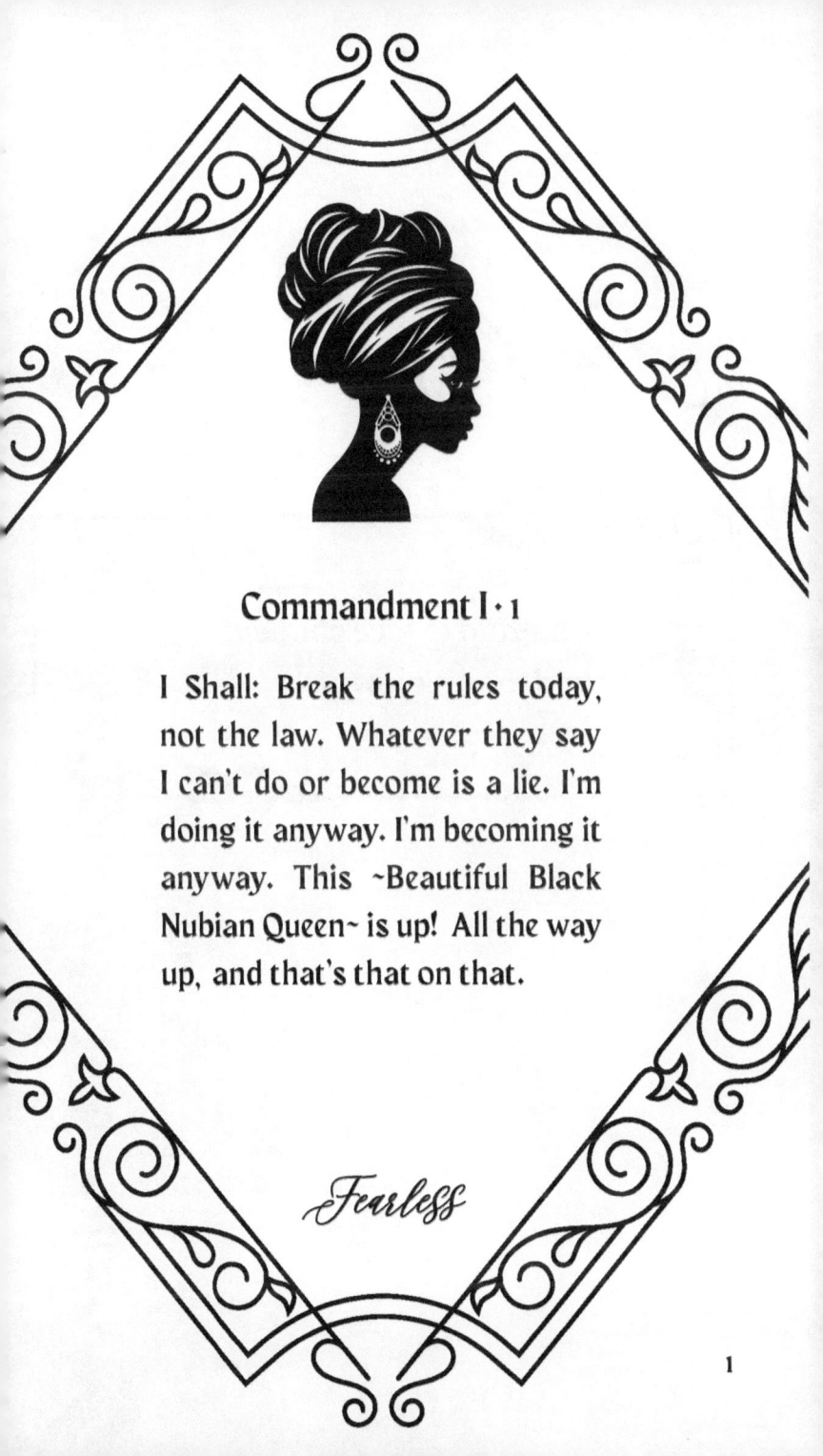

Commandment I · 1

I Shall: Break the rules today, not the law. Whatever they say I can't do or become is a lie. I'm doing it anyway. I'm becoming it anyway. This ~Beautiful Black Nubian Queen~ is up! All the way up, and that's that on that.

Fearless

Fearless

Unafraid to face challenges and the unknown.

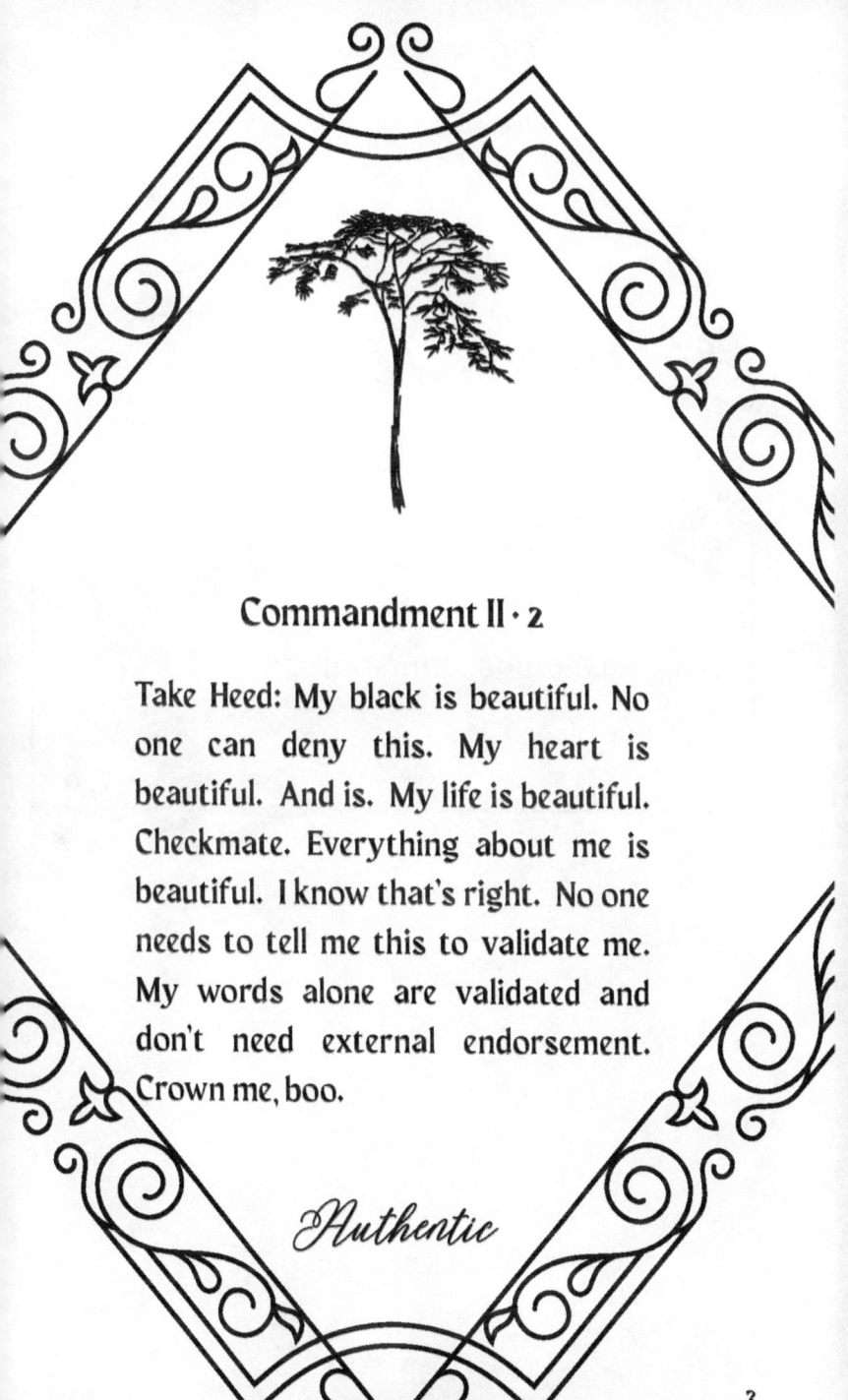

Commandment II · 2

Take Heed: My black is beautiful. No one can deny this. My heart is beautiful. And is. My life is beautiful. Checkmate. Everything about me is beautiful. I know that's right. No one needs to tell me this to validate me. My words alone are validated and don't need external endorsement. Crown me, boo.

Authentic

Authentic

Genuine, undisputedly real.

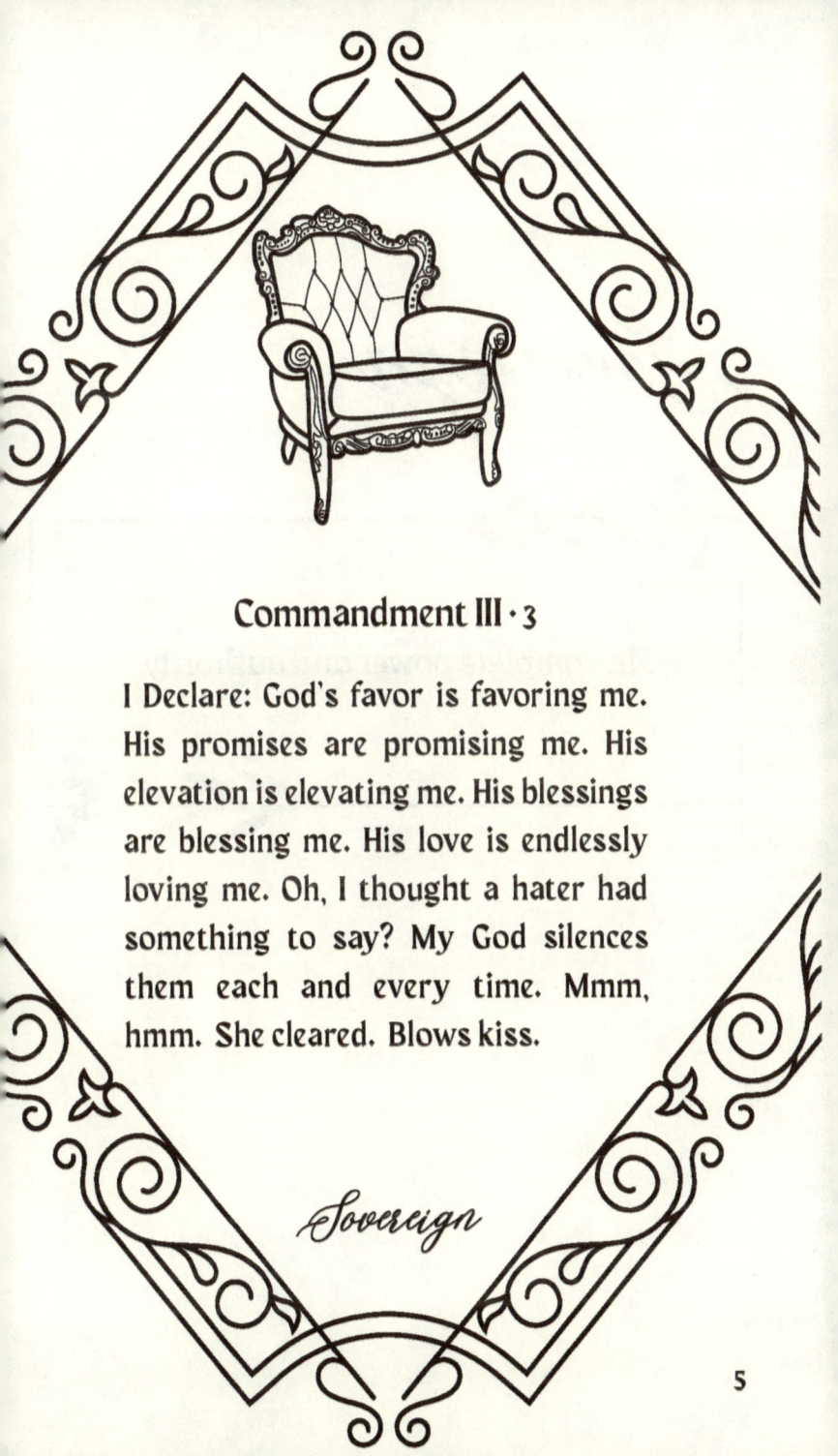

Commandment III · 3

I Declare: God's favor is favoring me. His promises are promising me. His elevation is elevating me. His blessings are blessing me. His love is endlessly loving me. Oh, I thought a hater had something to say? My God silences them each and every time. Mmm, hmm. She cleared. Blows kiss.

Sovereign

Sovereign

In complete power and authority.

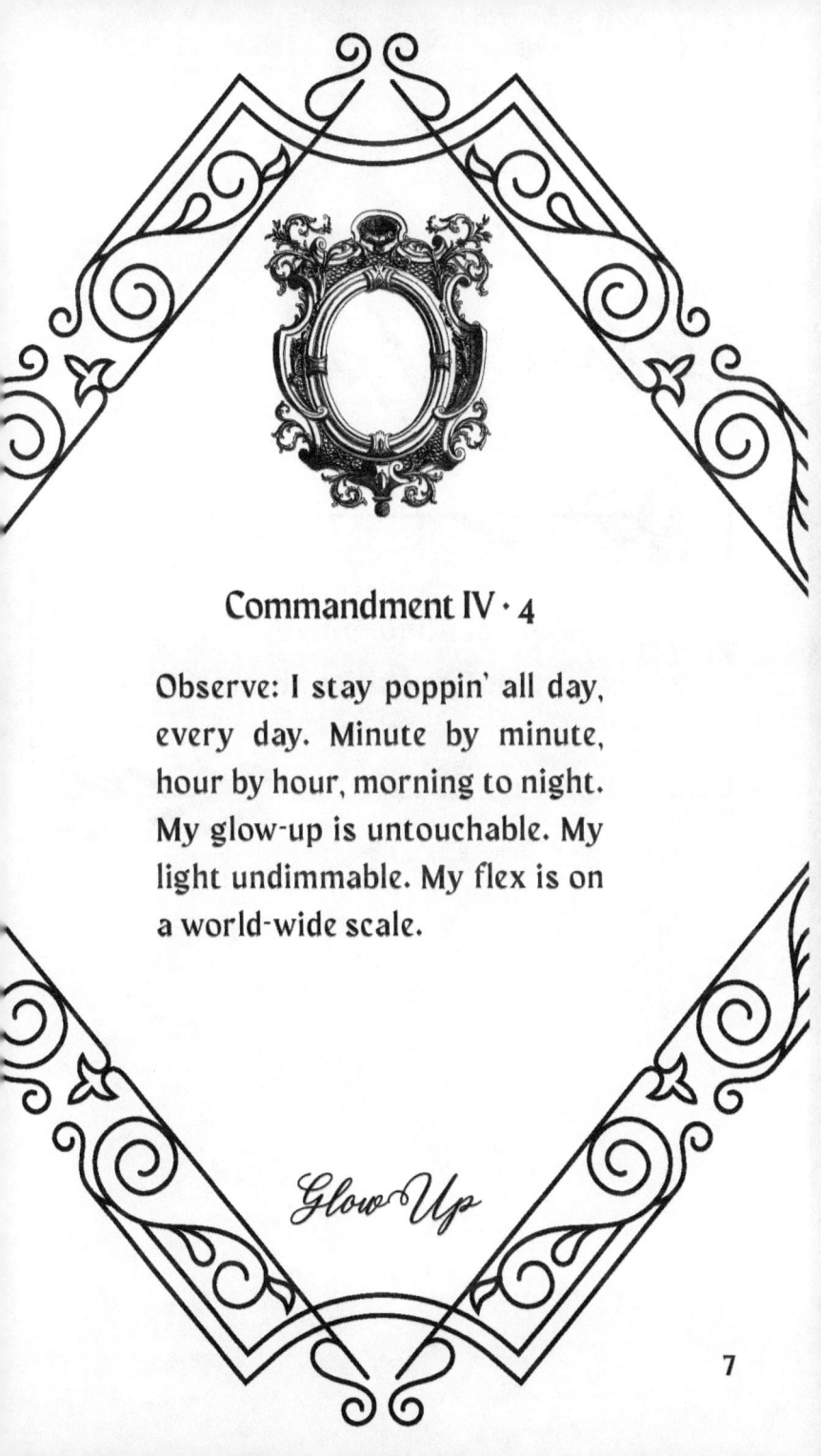

Commandment IV · 4

Observe: I stay poppin' all day, every day. Minute by minute, hour by hour, morning to night. My glow-up is untouchable. My light undimmable. My flex is on a world-wide scale.

Glow Up

Glow Up

Representing growth and
dramatic positive change.

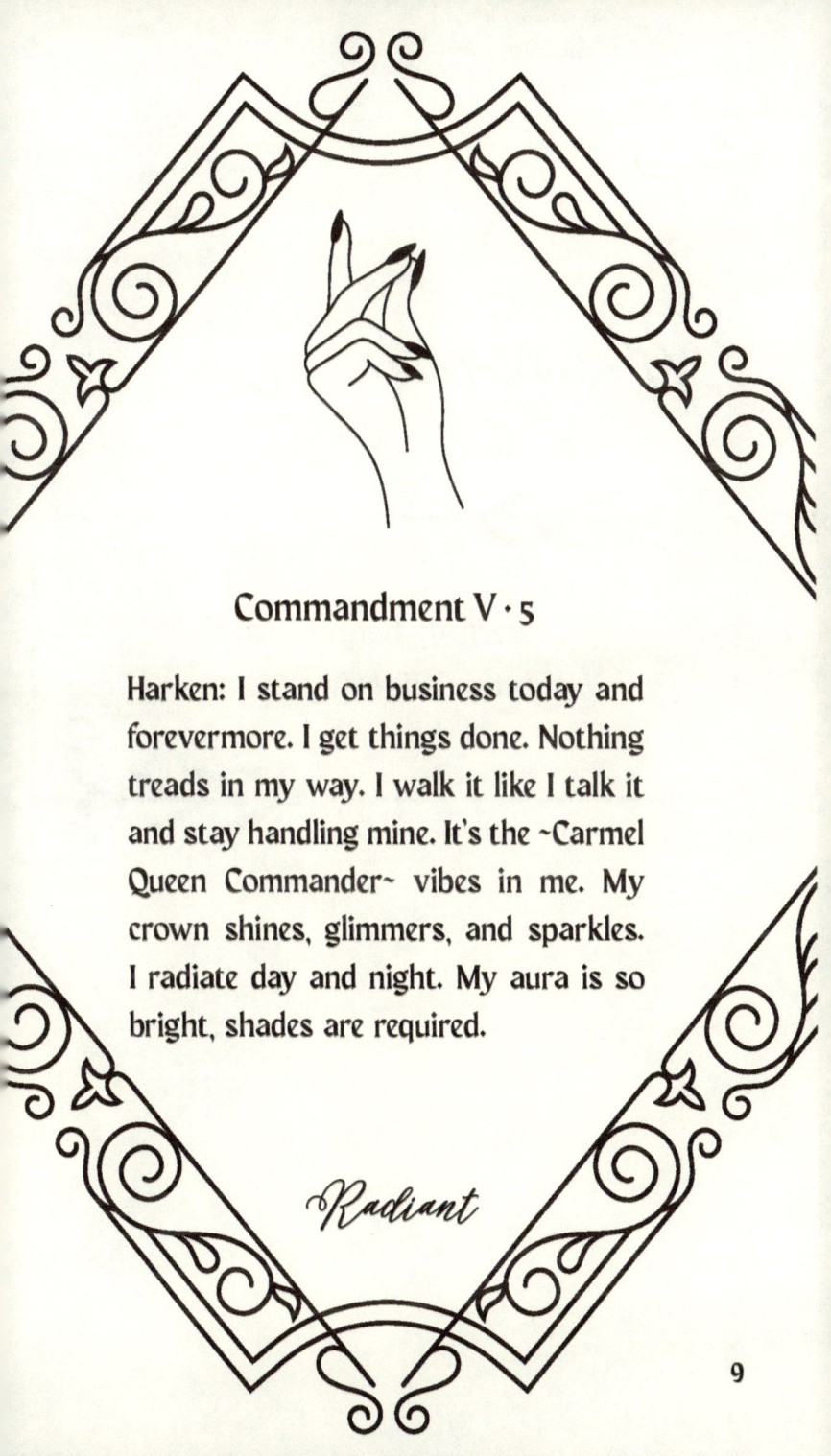

Commandment V · 5

Harken: I stand on business today and forevermore. I get things done. Nothing treads in my way. I walk it like I talk it and stay handling mine. It's the ~Carmel Queen Commander~ vibes in me. My crown shines, glimmers, and sparkles. I radiate day and night. My aura is so bright, shades are required.

Radiant

Radiant

Cheerfully beaming and shining brightly.

Commandment VI · 6

I Declare: I escape the mess. I block toxicity. No more disrespect. Less tension. A greater distance from lazy people. Heartbreakers removed. Liars on mute. Freed from energy vampires. Delivered from toil. Separated from those who keep trying my patience. My roots, strong. My cultural pride never hidden. My poise is on chill, and my ambition is on fire. I've got next.

Roots

Roots

*One's familial origins,
culture, and ancestry.*

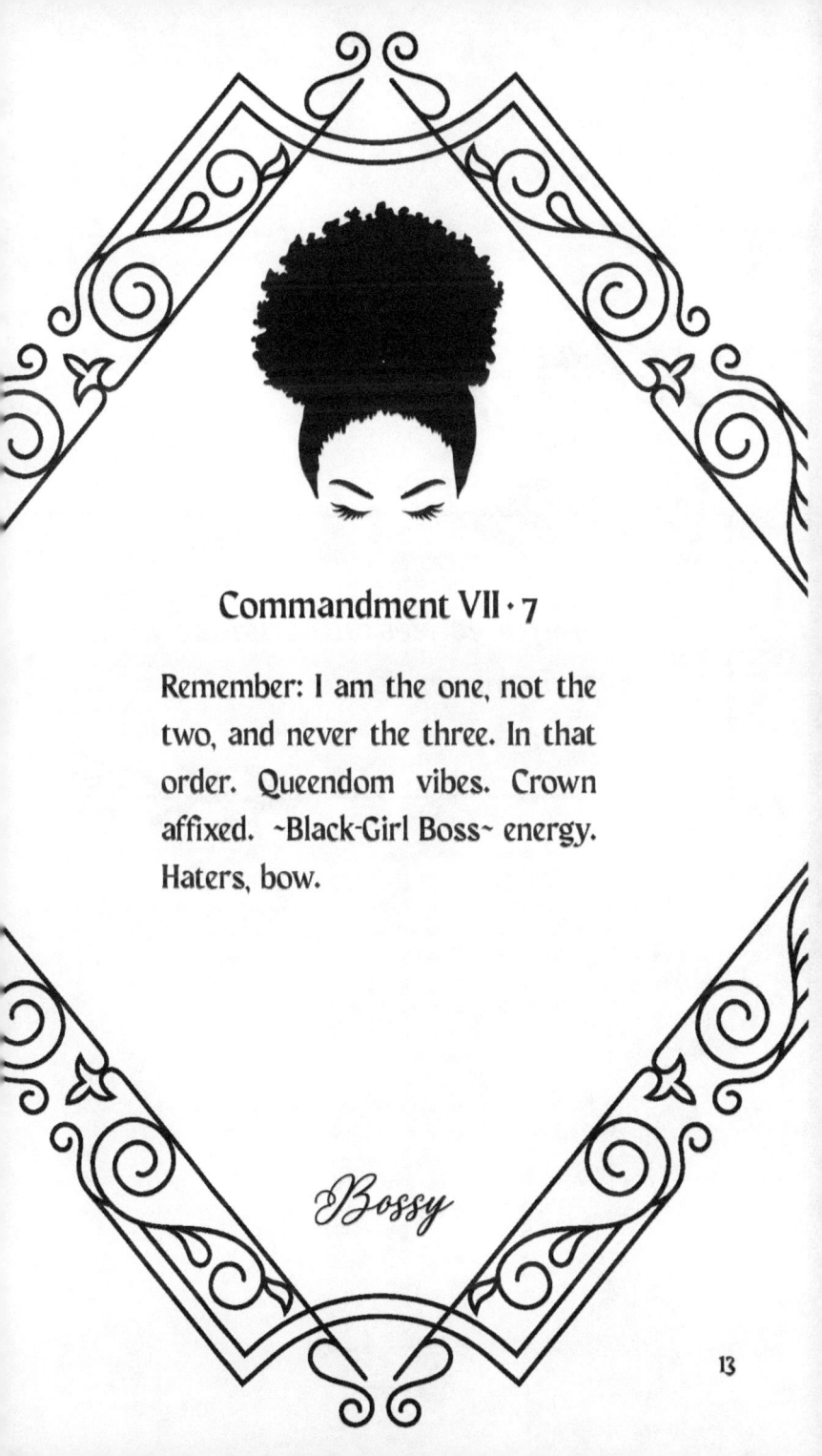

Commandment VII · 7

Remember: I am the one, not the two, and never the three. In that order. Queendom vibes. Crown affixed. ~Black-Girl Boss~ energy. Haters, bow.

Bossy

Bossy

Giving directives authoritatively, very domineering.

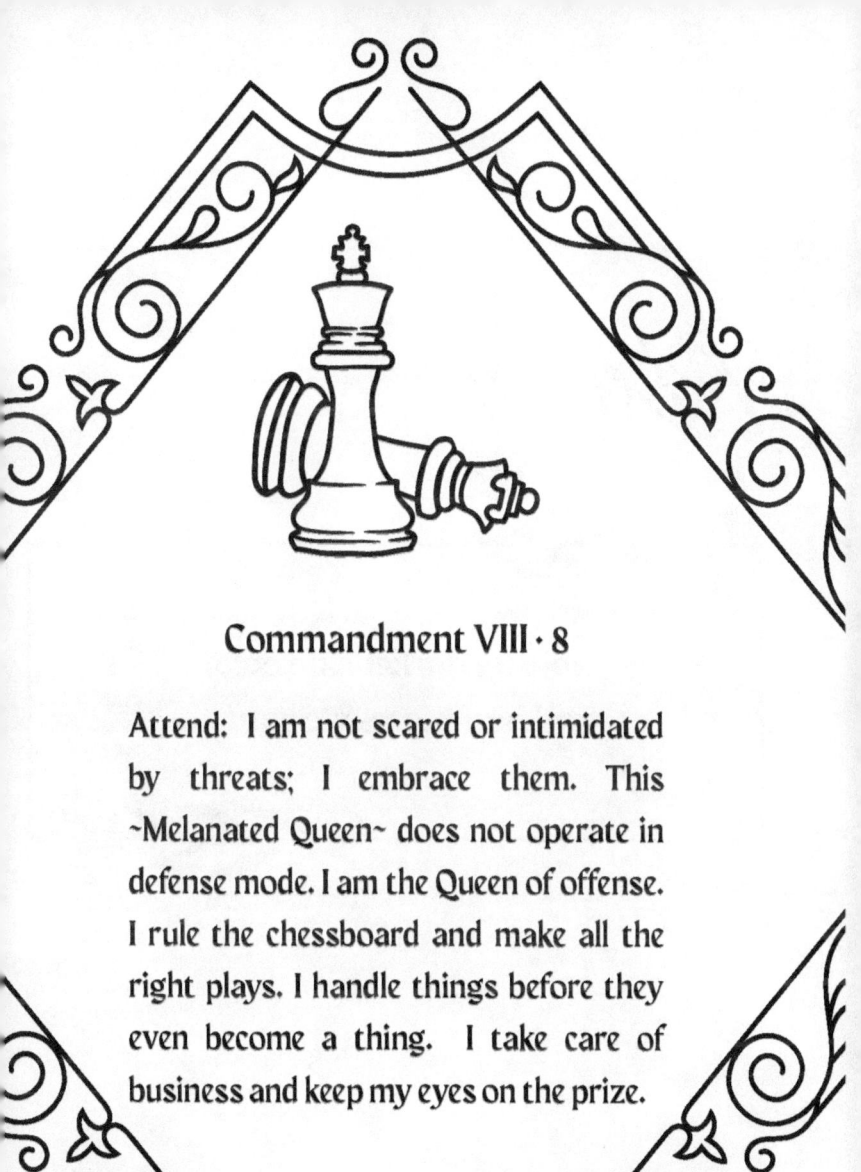

Commandment VIII · 8

Attend: I am not scared or intimidated by threats; I embrace them. This ~Melanated Queen~ does not operate in defense mode. I am the Queen of offense. I rule the chessboard and make all the right plays. I handle things before they even become a thing. I take care of business and keep my eyes on the prize.

Melanin

Melanin

Natural darker skin color and hair pigmentation.

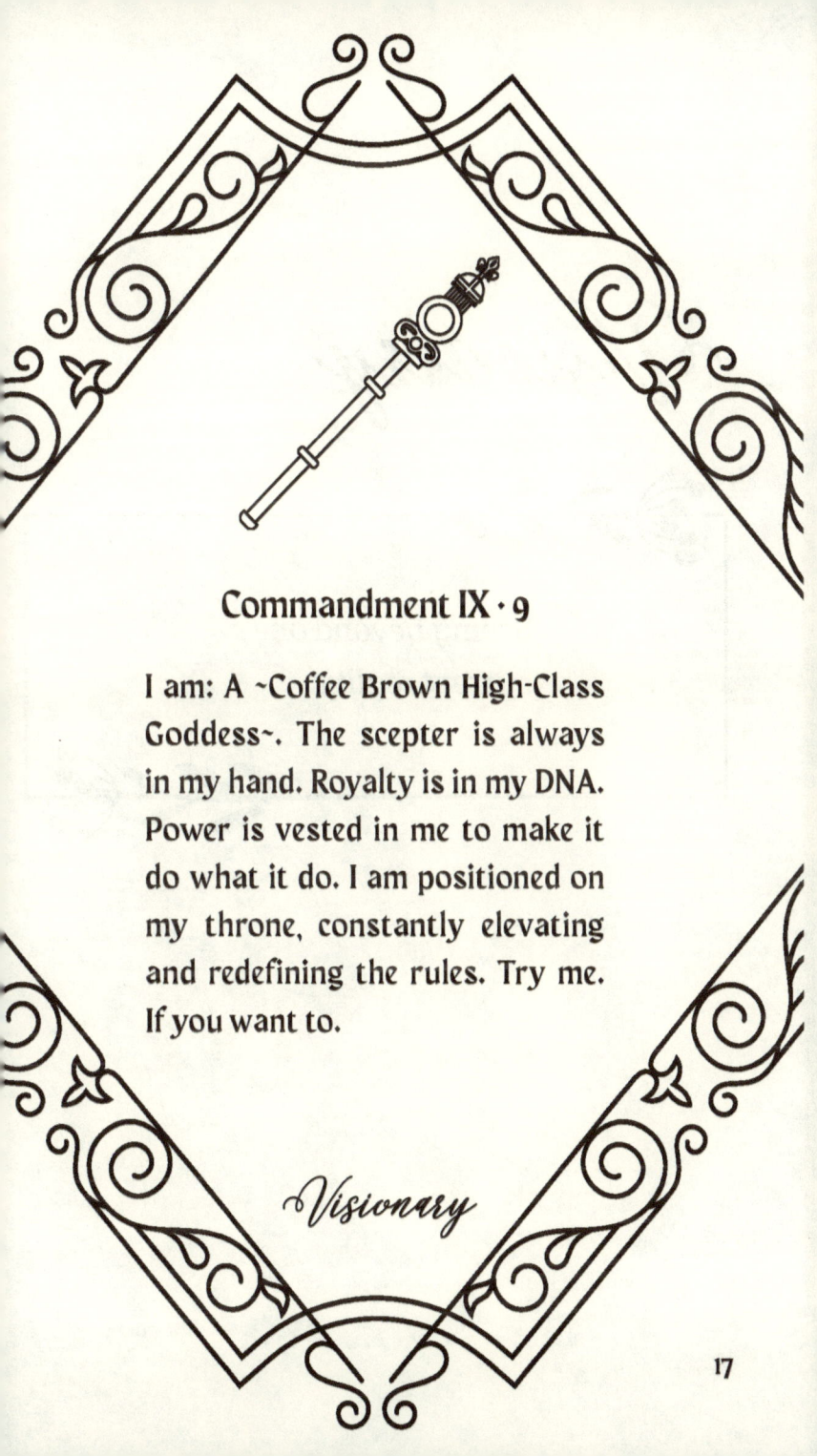

Commandment IX · 9

I am: A ~Coffee Brown High-Class Goddess~. The scepter is always in my hand. Royalty is in my DNA. Power is vested in me to make it do what it do. I am positioned on my throne, constantly elevating and redefining the rules. Try me. If you want to.

Visionary

Visionary

Seeing beyond one's current reality.

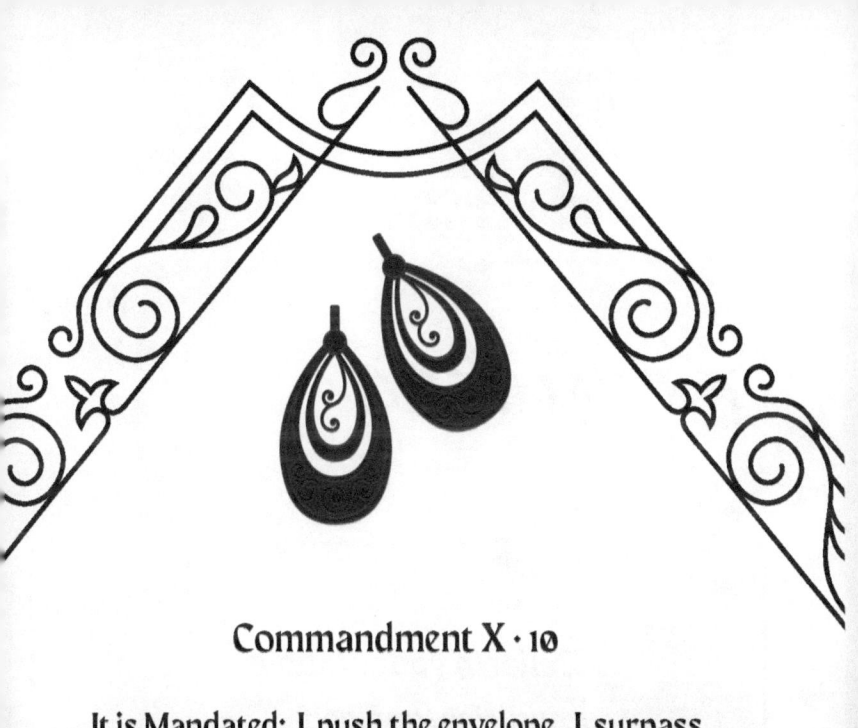

Commandment X · 10

It is Mandated: I push the envelope. I surpass the limits of societal norms. This ~Sista-Queen~ is bold and radical. I take risks. I innovate. I create. I develop. I deliver. I uncompromisingly rise to and above every occasion. My quantum-leap mindset is fully activated. I know that's right.

Confidence

Confidence

Belief in your abilities,
qualities, and self.

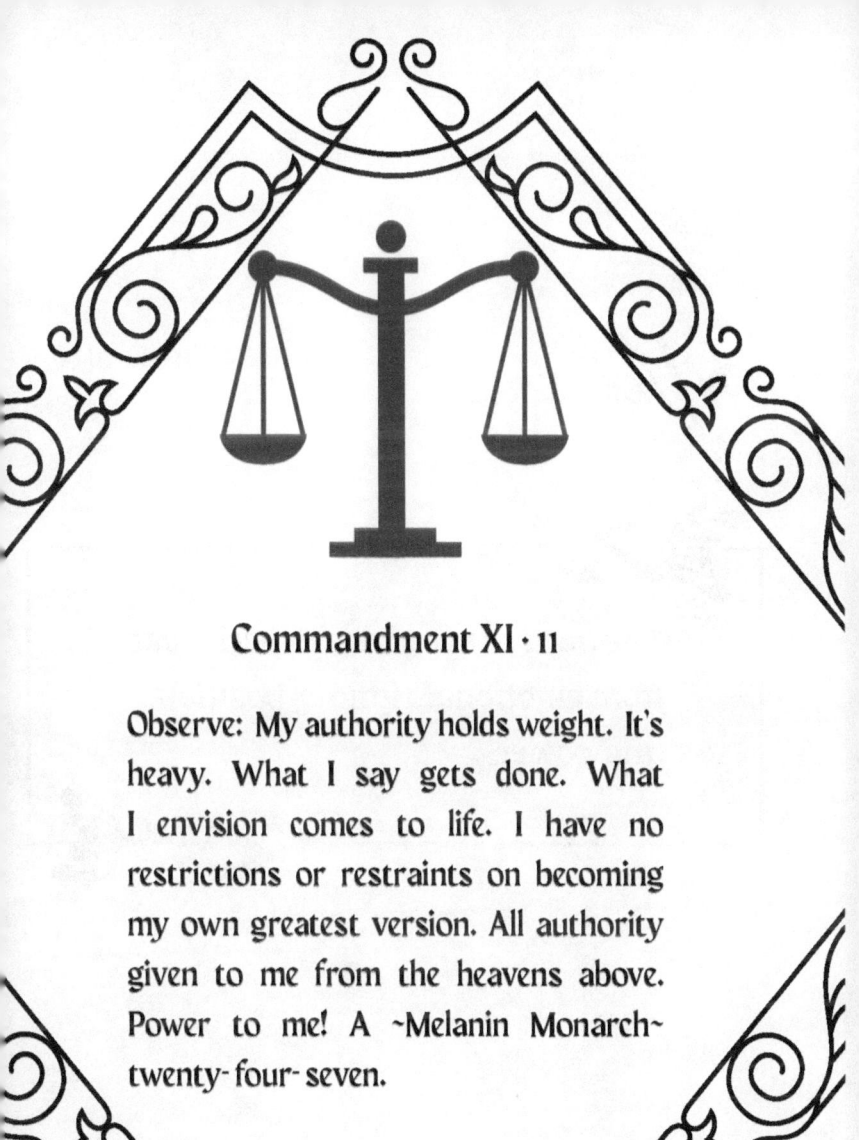

Commandment XI · 11

Observe: My authority holds weight. It's heavy. What I say gets done. What I envision comes to life. I have no restrictions or restraints on becoming my own greatest version. All authority given to me from the heavens above. Power to me! A ~Melanin Monarch~ twenty- four- seven.

Vibe

Vibe

The aura or mood one experiences from emotional signals, position, and power.

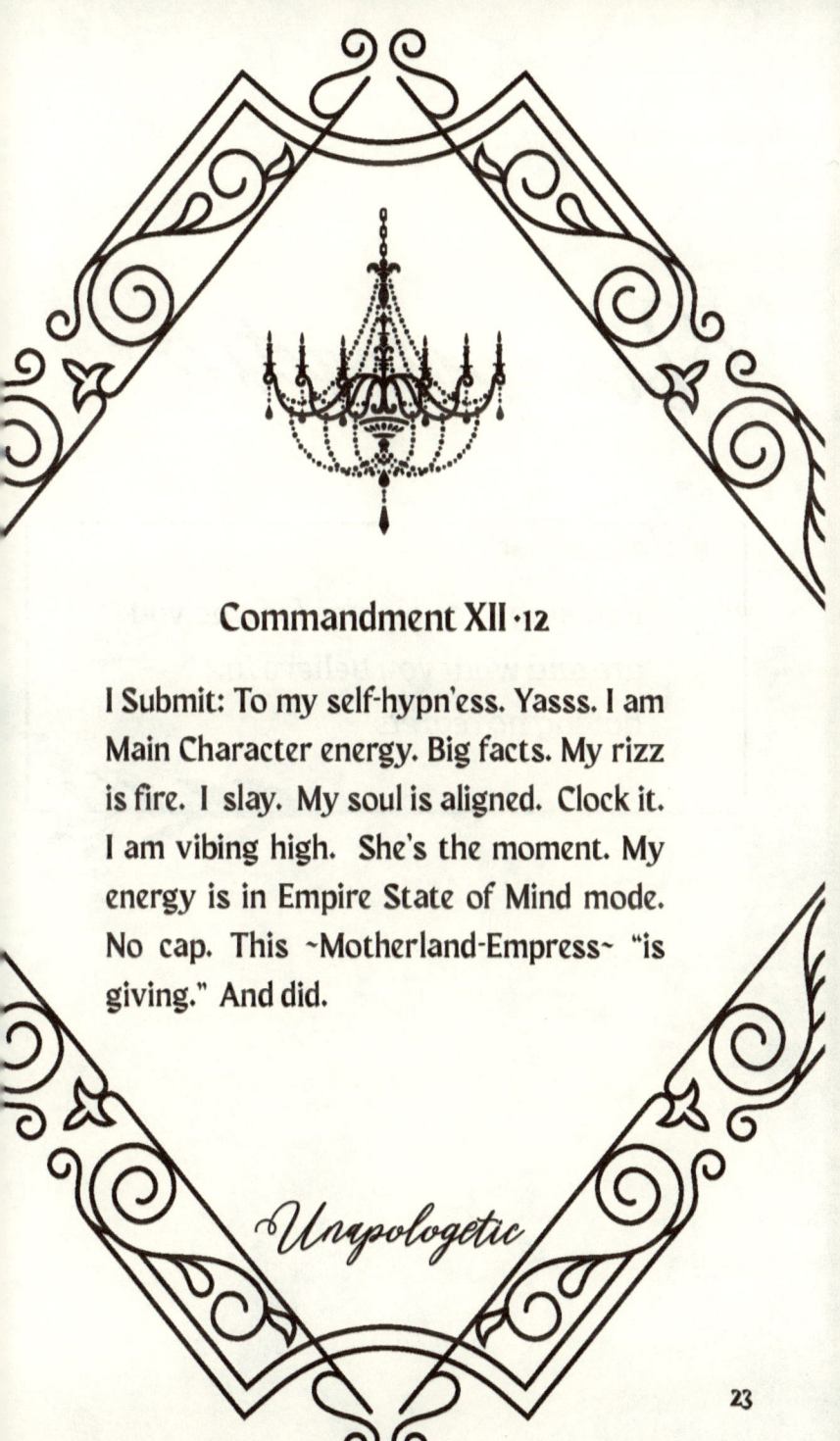

Commandment XII ·12

I Submit: To my self-hypn'ess. Yasss. I am Main Character energy. Big facts. My rizz is fire. I slay. My soul is aligned. Clock it. I am vibing high. She's the moment. My energy is in Empire State of Mind mode. No cap. This ~Motherland-Empress~ "is giving." And did.

Unapologetic

Unapologetic

Refusing to apologize for who you are and what you believe in, having no regrets.

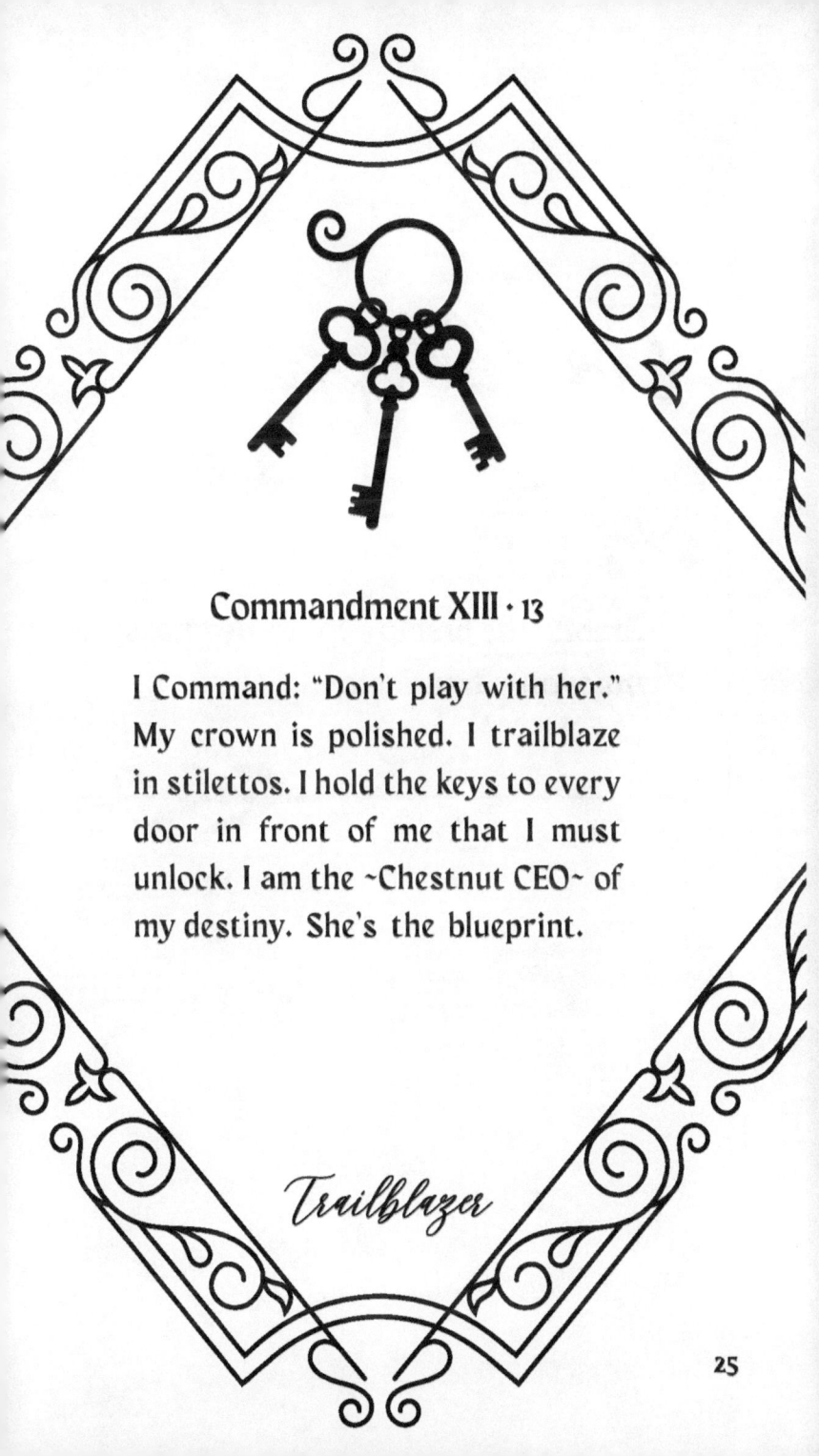

Commandment XIII · 13

I Command: "Don't play with her."
My crown is polished. I trailblaze
in stilettos. I hold the keys to every
door in front of me that I must
unlock. I am the ~Chestnut CEO~ of
my destiny. She's the blueprint.

Trailblazer

Trailblazer

Among the first to explore newness; innovator, trendsetter.

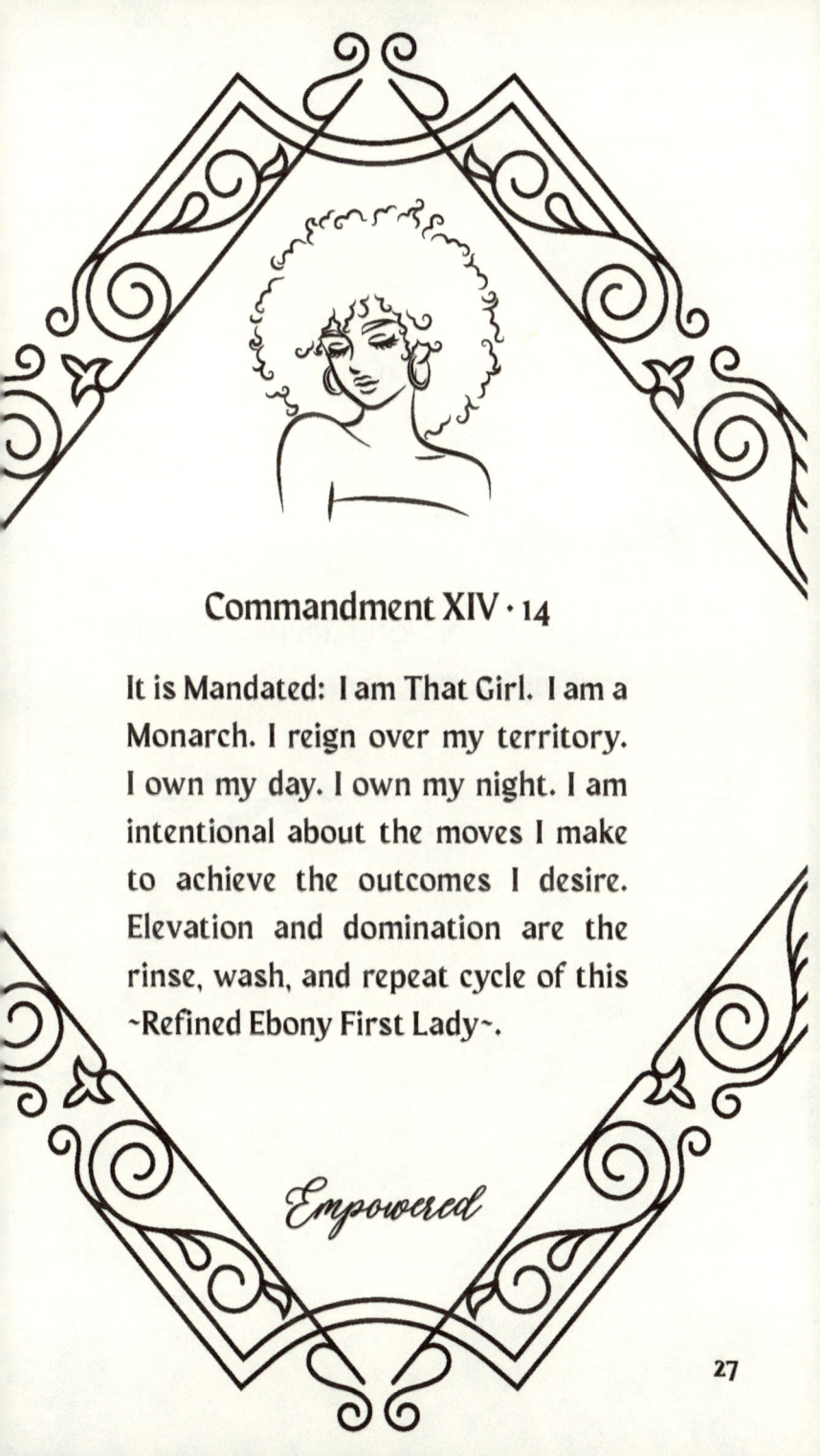

Commandment XIV · 14

It is Mandated: I am That Girl. I am a Monarch. I reign over my territory. I own my day. I own my night. I am intentional about the moves I make to achieve the outcomes I desire. Elevation and domination are the rinse, wash, and repeat cycle of this ~Refined Ebony First Lady~.

Empowered

Empowered

Assured in making decisions and making moves for oneself.

Commandment XV · 15

Honor: "I am every woman." It is truly all in me. This is understood. And what's understood, I do not have to explain or defend ever. Period.

Queen

Queen

A woman who rules a kingdom.

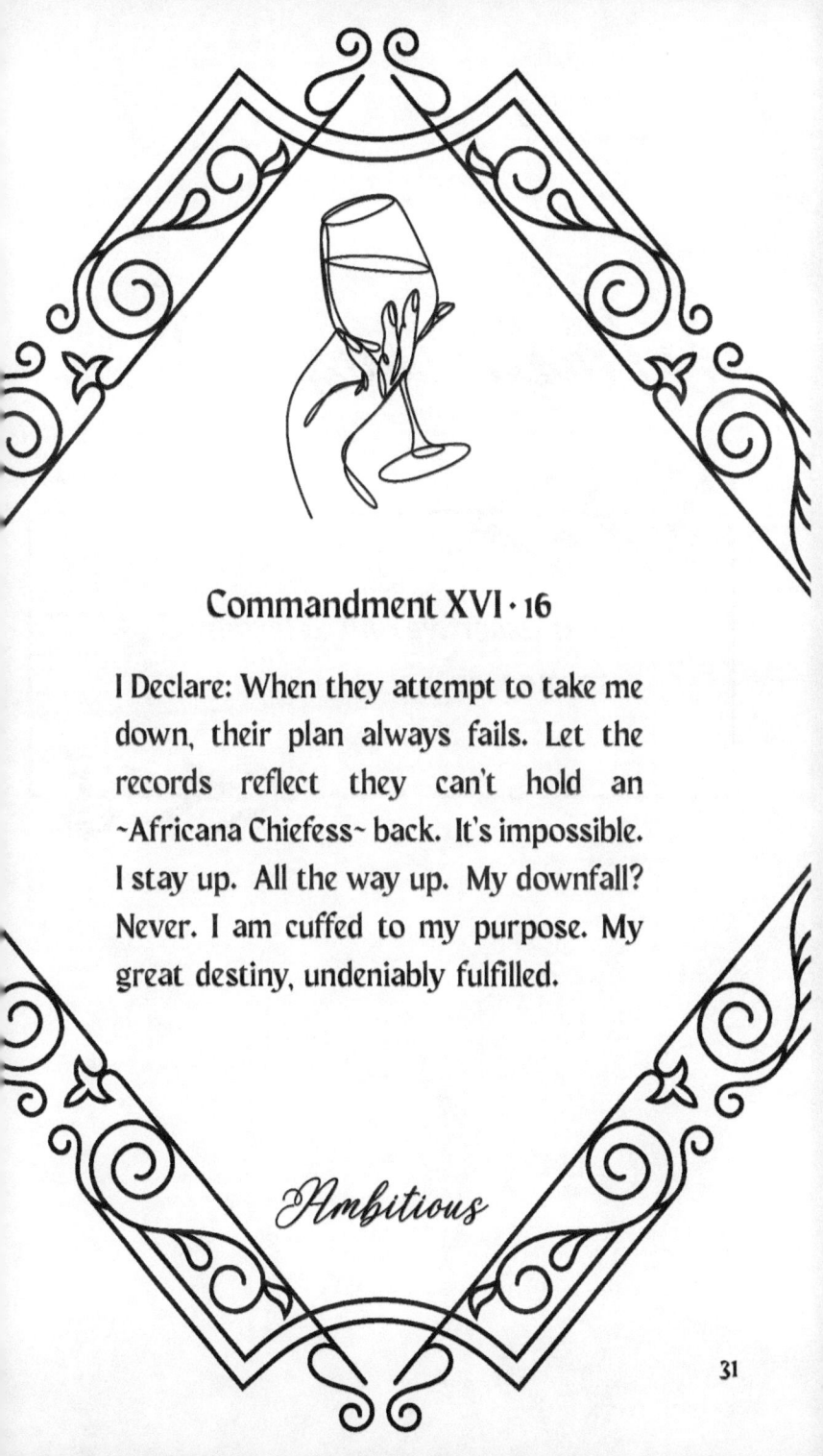

Commandment XVI · 16

I Declare: When they attempt to take me down, their plan always fails. Let the records reflect they can't hold an ~Africana Chiefess~ back. It's impossible. I stay up. All the way up. My downfall? Never. I am cuffed to my purpose. My great destiny, undeniably fulfilled.

Ambitious

Ambitious

Self-assertive and determined
to succeed.

Commandment XVII · 17

Harken: No one comes for me unless I send for them, and I don't send for them. I protect my heart. I protect my soul. This ~Caramel Regal~ summons only glow-up, soft life, and success. Soulful strategy in action.

Bold

Bold

Gallant, unblushing, resistant to opposition.

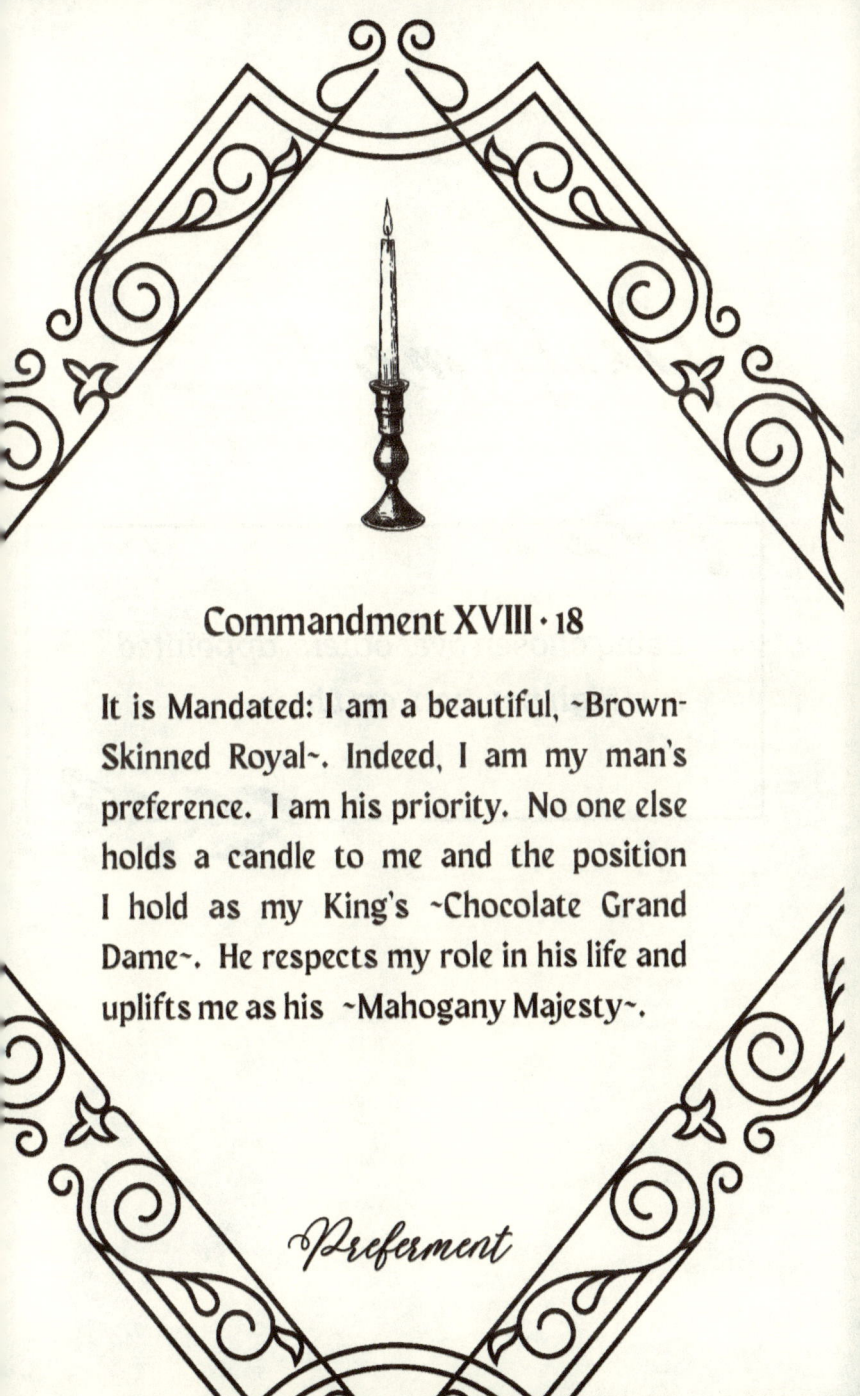

Commandment XVIII · 18

It is Mandated: I am a beautiful, ~Brown-Skinned Royal~. Indeed, I am my man's preference. I am his priority. No one else holds a candle to me and the position I hold as my King's ~Chocolate Grand Dame~. He respects my role in his life and uplifts me as his ~Mahogany Majesty~.

Preferment

Preferment

Being chosen over others, appointed
to a high position, and honor.

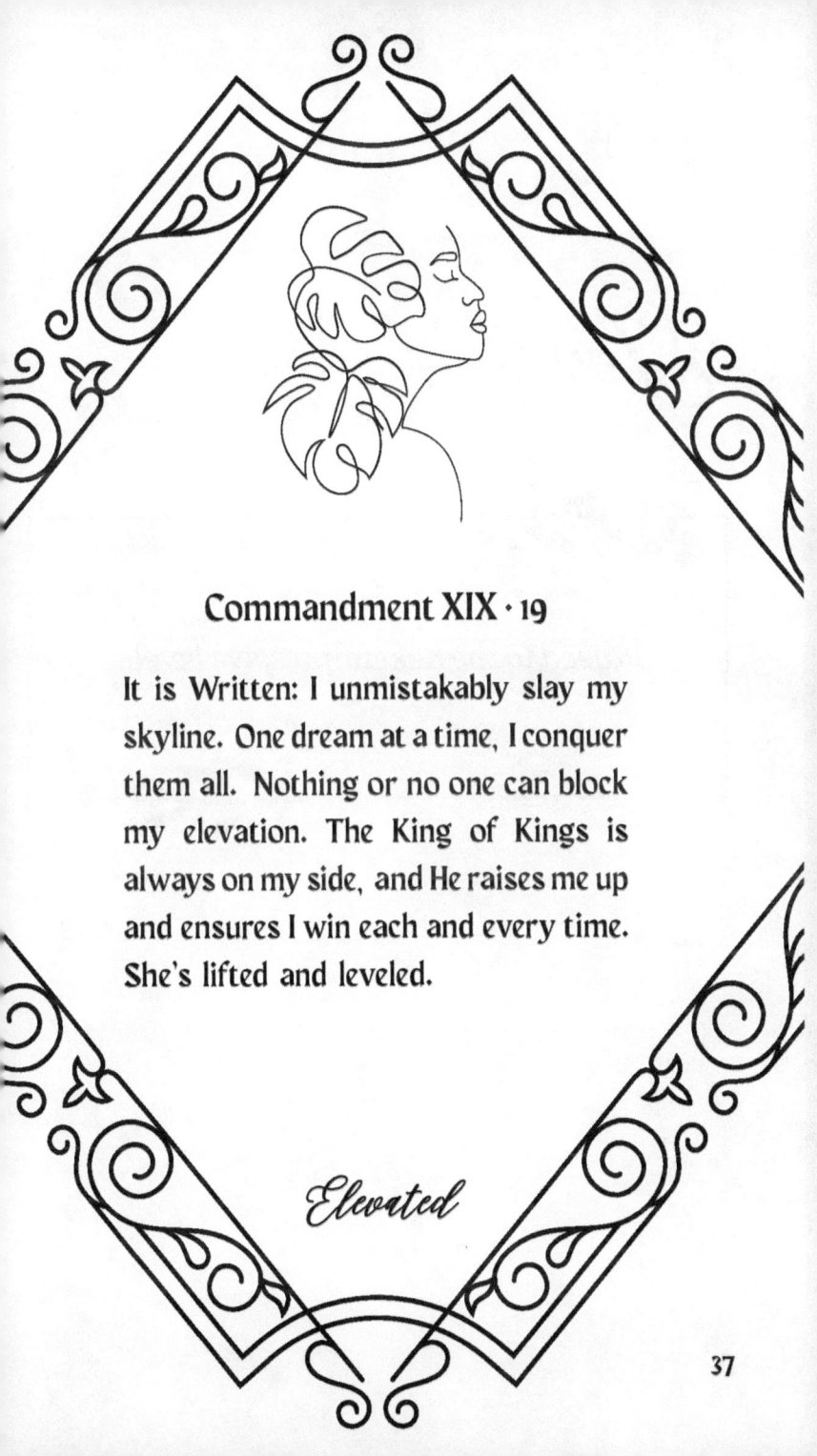

Commandment XIX · 19

It is Written: I unmistakably slay my skyline. One dream at a time, I conquer them all. Nothing or no one can block my elevation. The King of Kings is always on my side, and He raises me up and ensures I win each and every time. She's lifted and leveled.

Elevated

Elevated

Raised to the next impressive level.

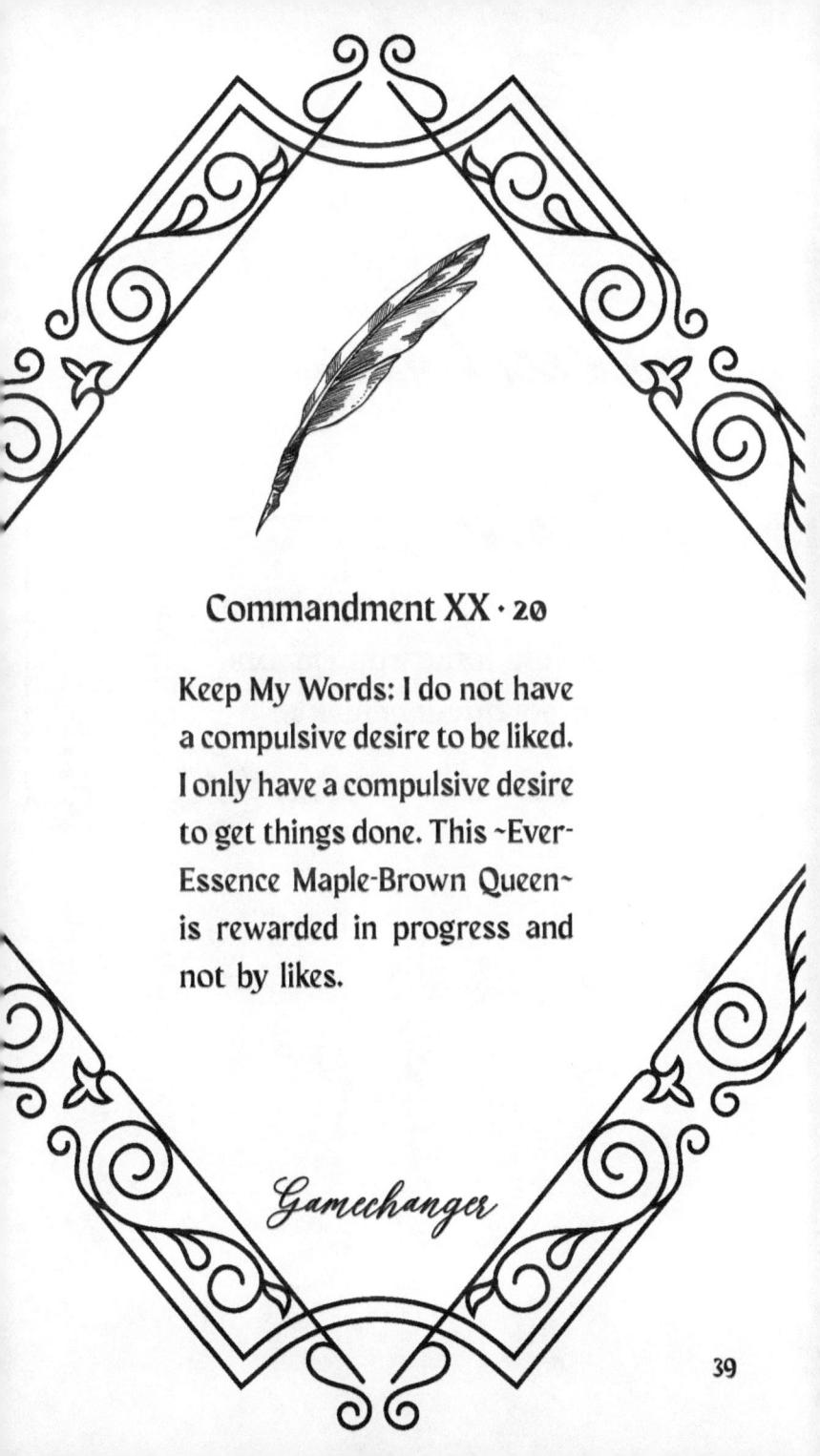

Commandment XX · 20

Keep My Words: I do not have a compulsive desire to be liked. I only have a compulsive desire to get things done. This ~Ever-Essence Maple-Brown Queen~ is rewarded in progress and not by likes.

Gamechanger

Gamechanger

Someone or something that is revolutionary and favors major advancements.

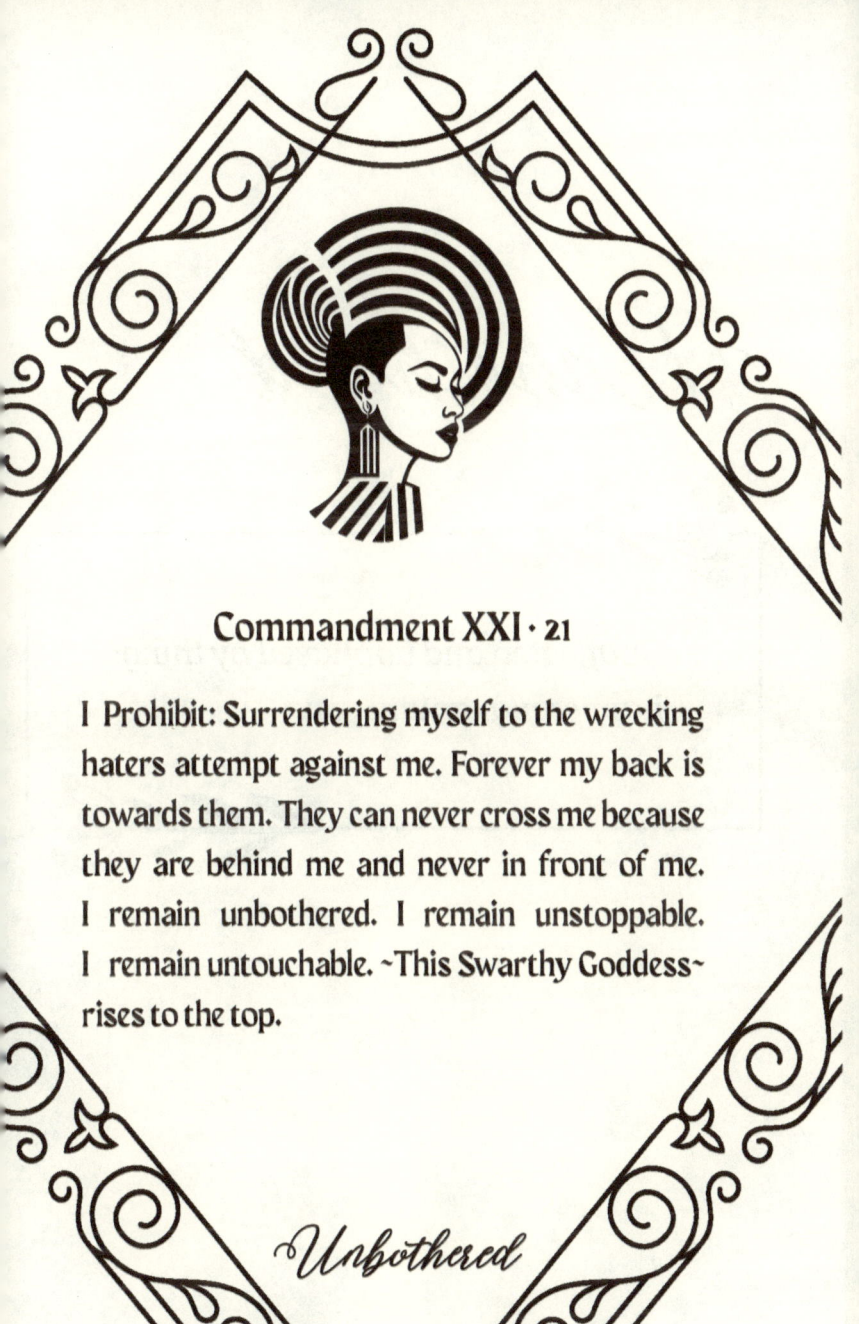

Commandment XXI · 21

I Prohibit: Surrendering myself to the wrecking haters attempt against me. Forever my back is towards them. They can never cross me because they are behind me and never in front of me. I remain unbothered. I remain unstoppable. I remain untouchable. ~This Swarthy Goddess~ rises to the top.

Unbothered

Unbothered

Unaffected and unphased by things
happening around you.

Commandment XXII · 22

Harken: What I say is done. The words that proceed from the mouth of this benevolent, ~Cinnamon-Toasted Enchantress~ prevail always. Every delightful word I speak holds power and comes to life. My words are resplendent to my viability. They are luminous to my life. They are elaborate to my actuality. My words do exactly what I say when I say them.

Luminary

Luminary

A notable person with superstardom.

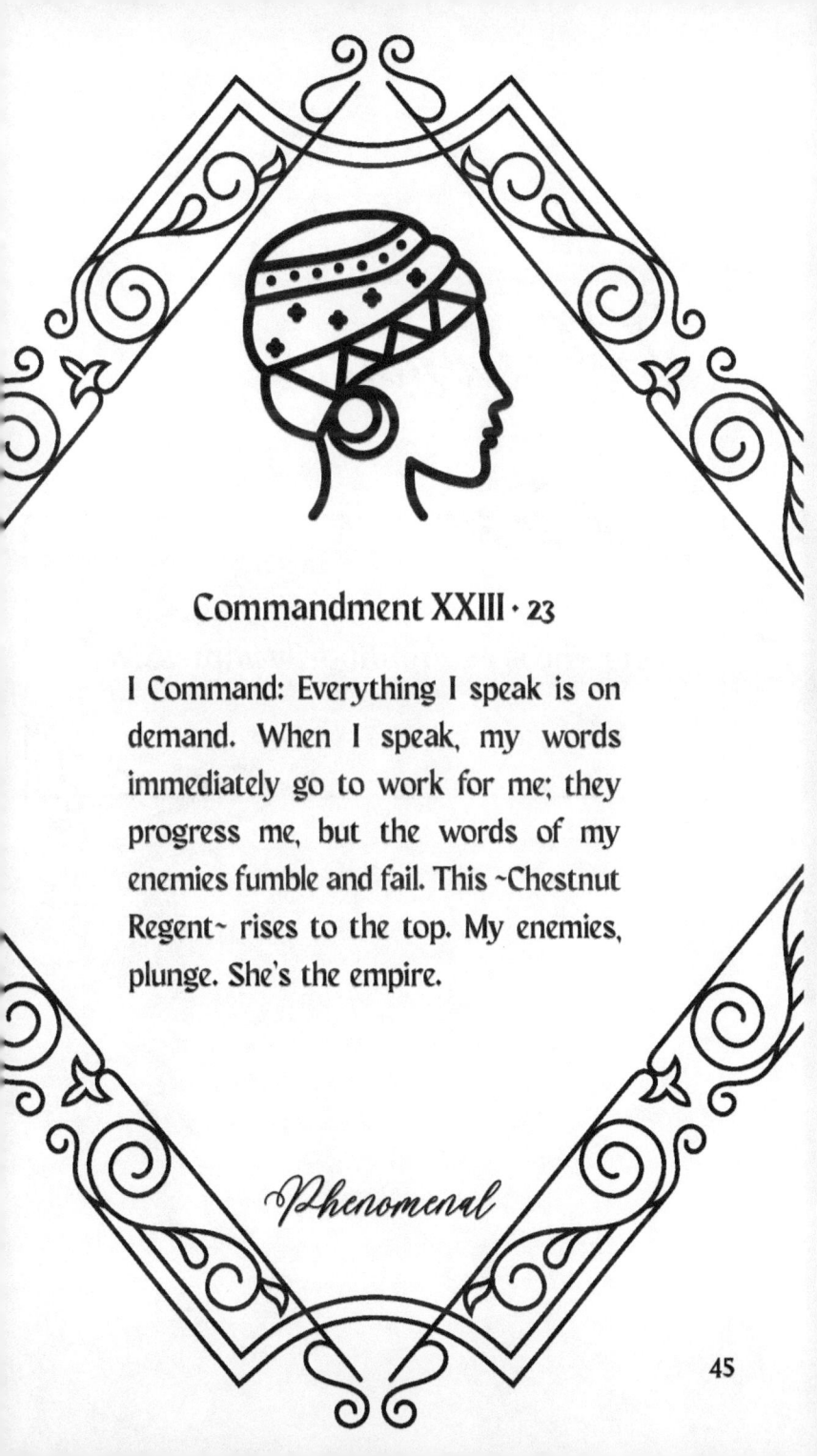

Commandment XXIII · 23

I Command: Everything I speak is on demand. When I speak, my words immediately go to work for me; they progress me, but the words of my enemies fumble and fail. This ~Chestnut Regent~ rises to the top. My enemies, plunge. She's the empire.

Phenomenal

Phenomenal

One who is extraordinarily impressive.

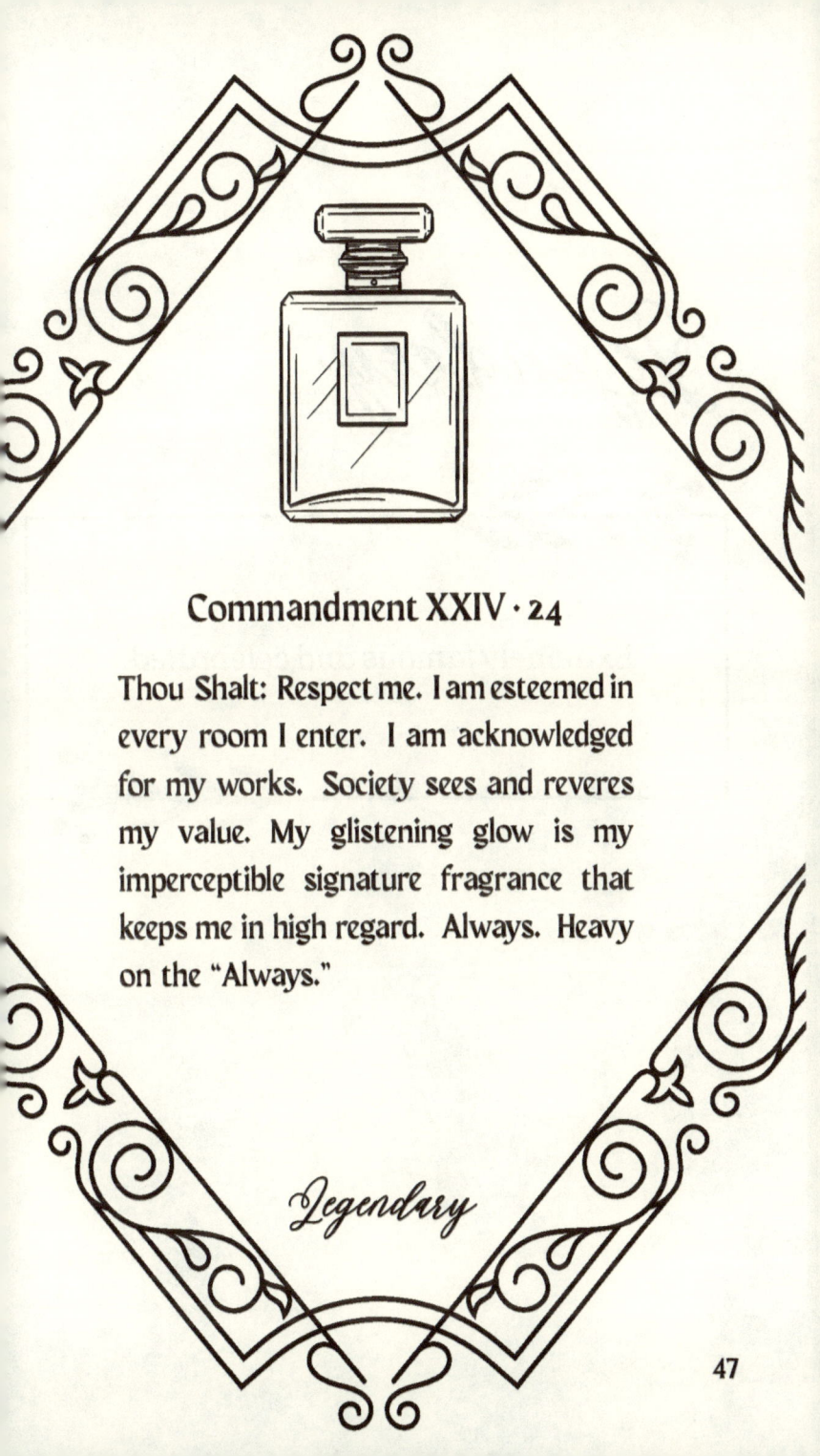

Commandment XXIV · 24

Thou Shalt: Respect me. I am esteemed in every room I enter. I am acknowledged for my works. Society sees and reveres my value. My glistening glow is my imperceptible signature fragrance that keeps me in high regard. Always. Heavy on the "Always."

Legendary

Legendary

Extremely famous and celebrated.

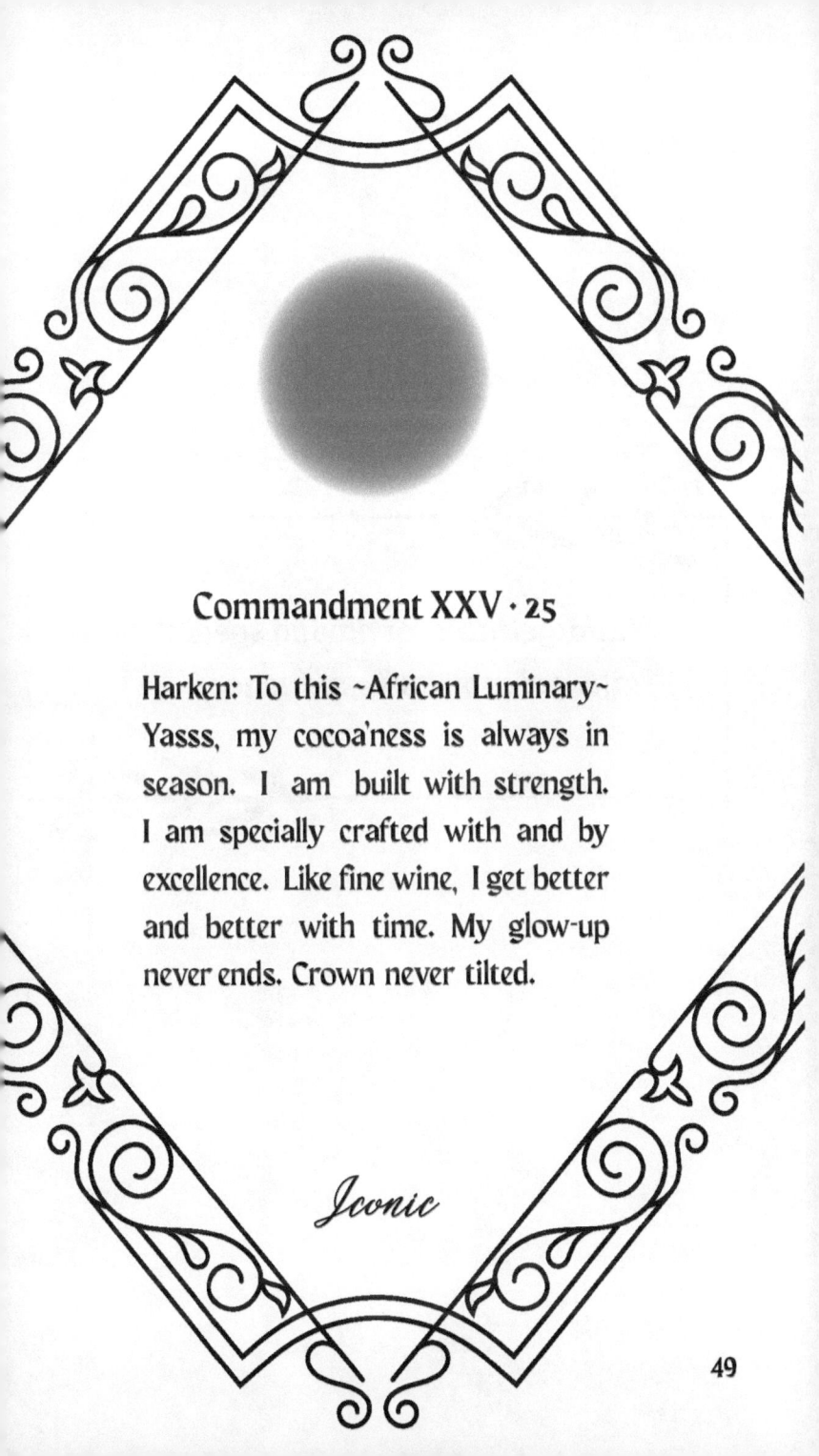

Commandment XXV · 25

Harken: To this ~African Luminary~ Yasss, my cocoa'ness is always in season. I am built with strength. I am specially crafted with and by excellence. Like fine wine, I get better and better with time. My glow-up never ends. Crown never tilted.

Iconic

Iconic

Unforgettable for having special gifts, talents, and experiences.

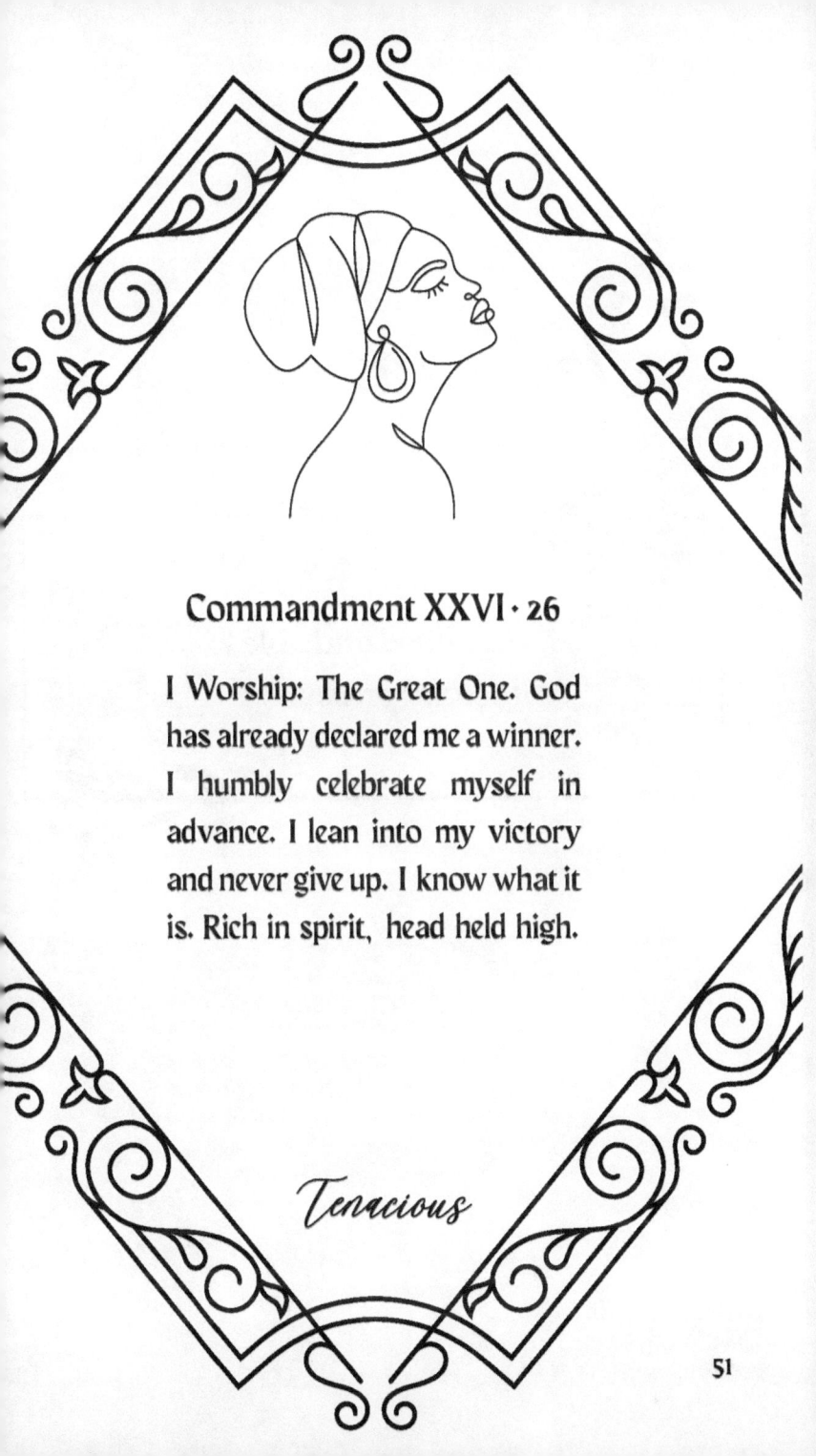

Commandment XXVI · 26

I Worship: The Great One. God
has already declared me a winner.
I humbly celebrate myself in
advance. I lean into my victory
and never give up. I know what it
is. Rich in spirit, head held high.

Tenacious

Tenacious

Determined and able to
withstand pressure.

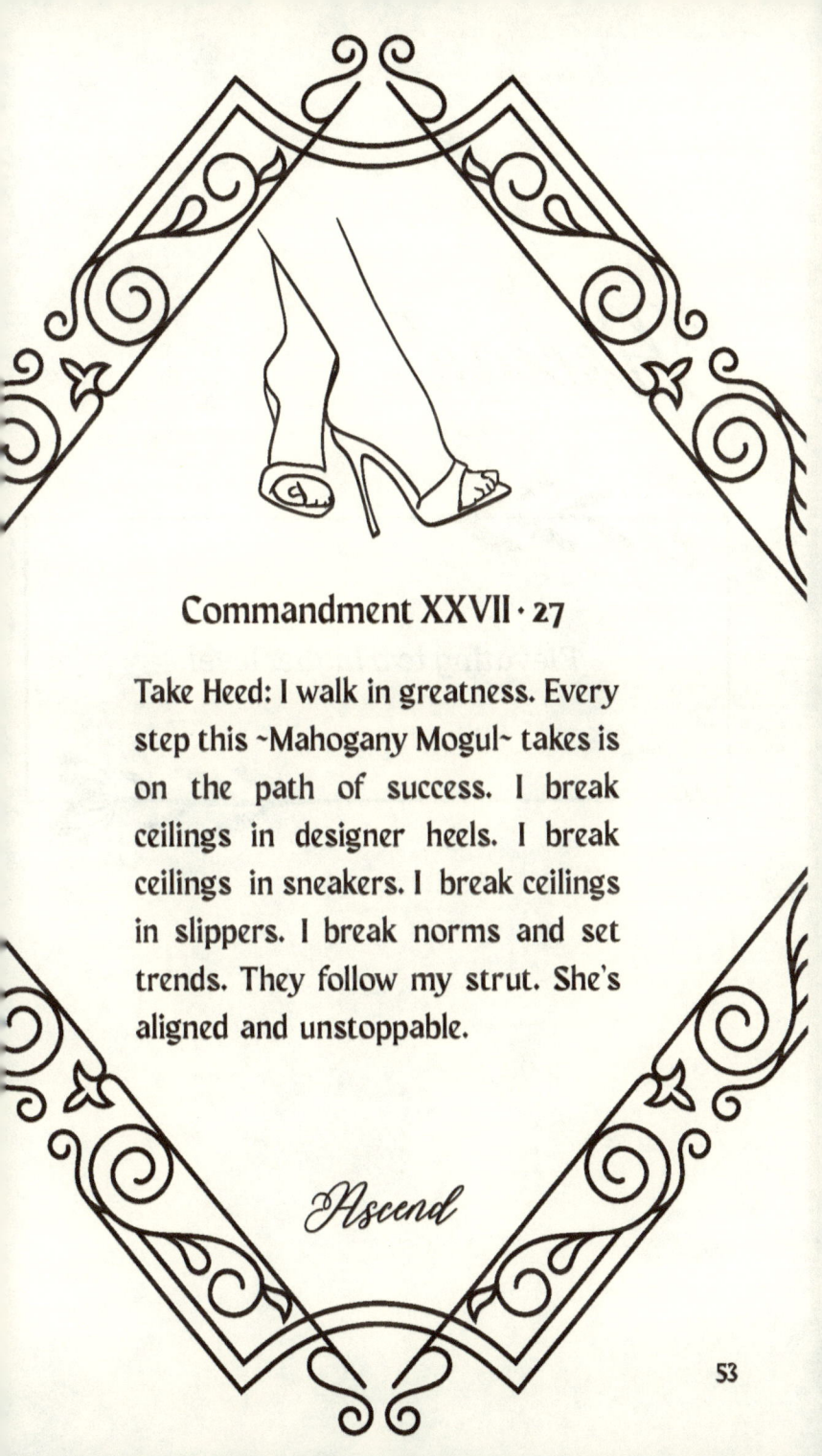

Commandment XXVII · 27

Take Heed: I walk in greatness. Every step this ~Mahogany Mogul~ takes is on the path of success. I break ceilings in designer heels. I break ceilings in sneakers. I break ceilings in slippers. I break norms and set trends. They follow my strut. She's aligned and unstoppable.

Ascend

Ascend

Elevating to a higher level.

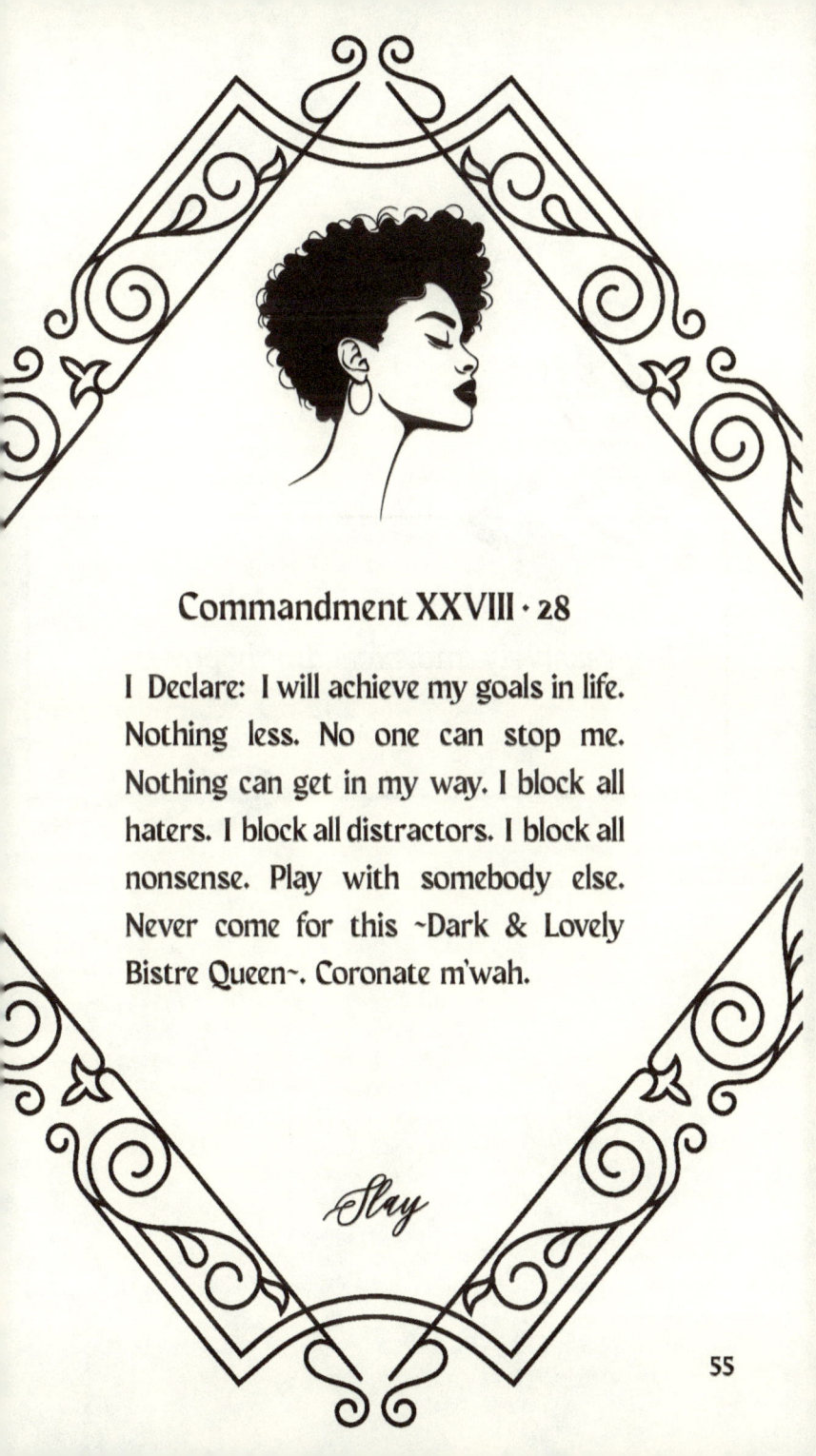

Commandment XXVIII · 28

I Declare: I will achieve my goals in life. Nothing less. No one can stop me. Nothing can get in my way. I block all haters. I block all distractors. I block all nonsense. Play with somebody else. Never come for this ~Dark & Lovely Bistre Queen~. Coronate m'wah.

Slay

Slay

Impressively and exceedingly powerful.

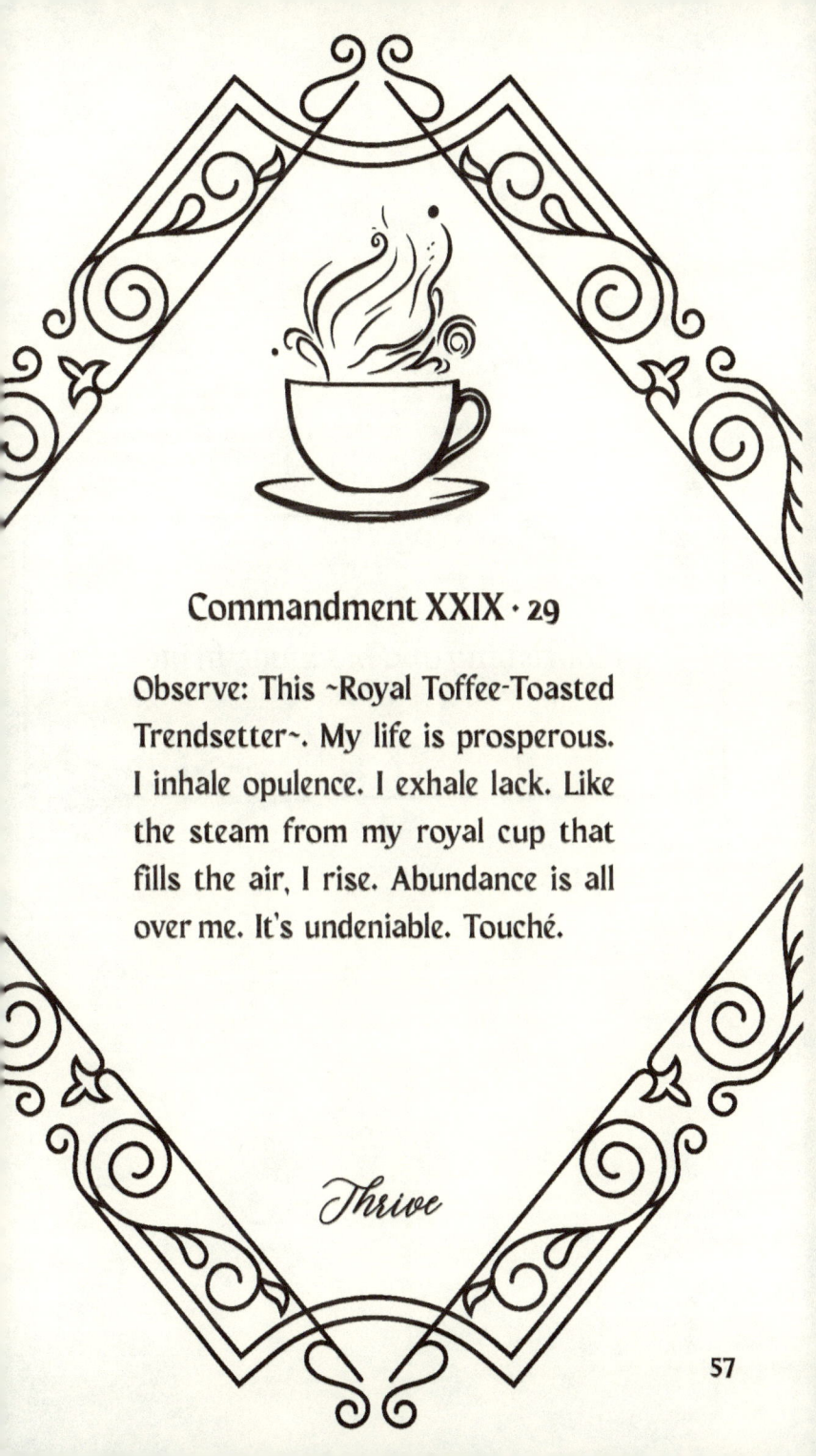

Commandment XXIX · 29

Observe: This ~Royal Toffee-Toasted Trendsetter~. My life is prosperous. I inhale opulence. I exhale lack. Like the steam from my royal cup that fills the air, I rise. Abundance is all over me. It's undeniable. Touché.

Thrive

Thrive

Flourishing and blooming in life.

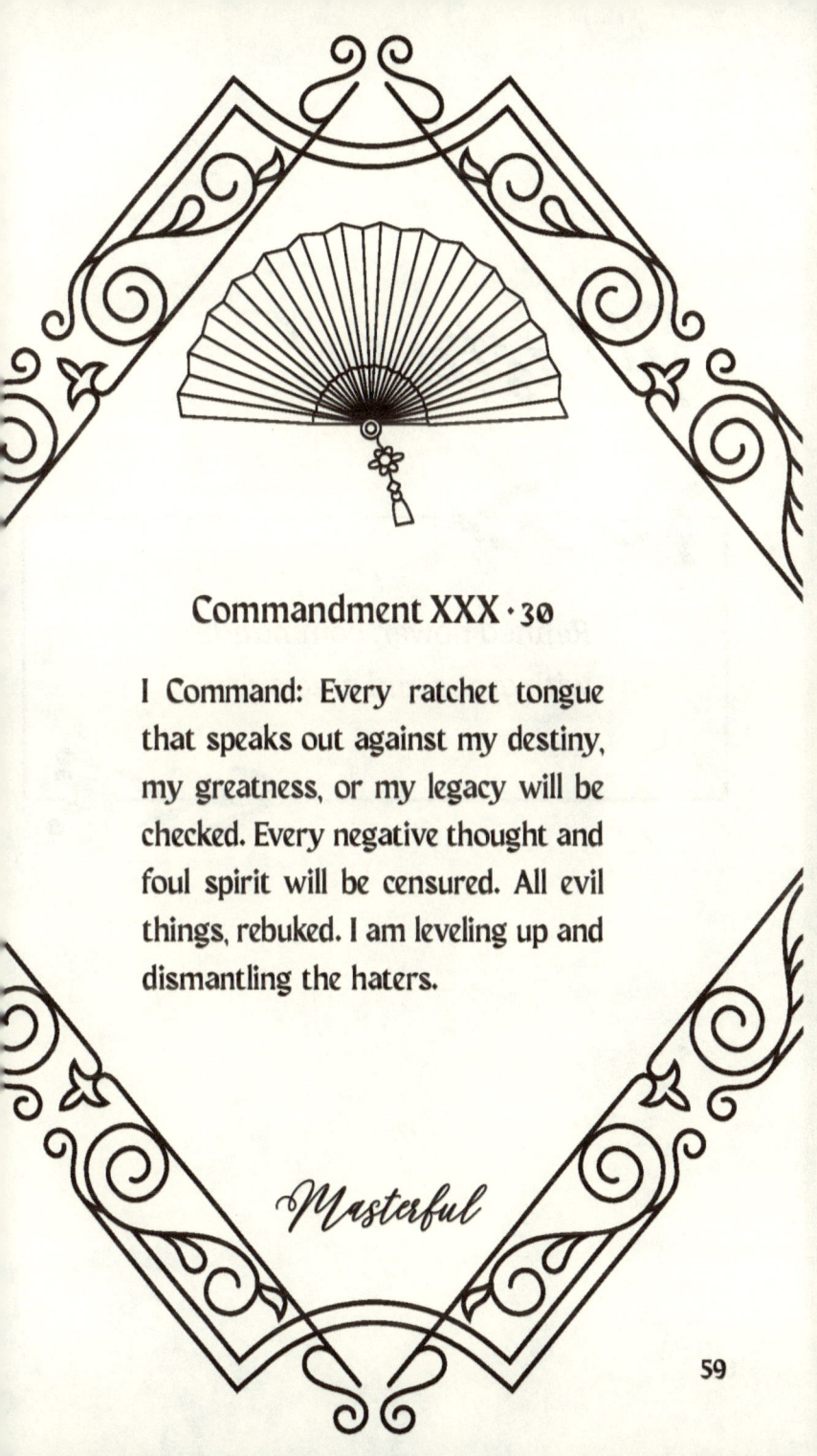

Commandment XXX · 30

I Command: Every ratchet tongue that speaks out against my destiny, my greatness, or my legacy will be checked. Every negative thought and foul spirit will be censured. All evil things, rebuked. I am leveling up and dismantling the haters.

Masterful

Masterful

*Refined power, commanding
with grace and precision.*

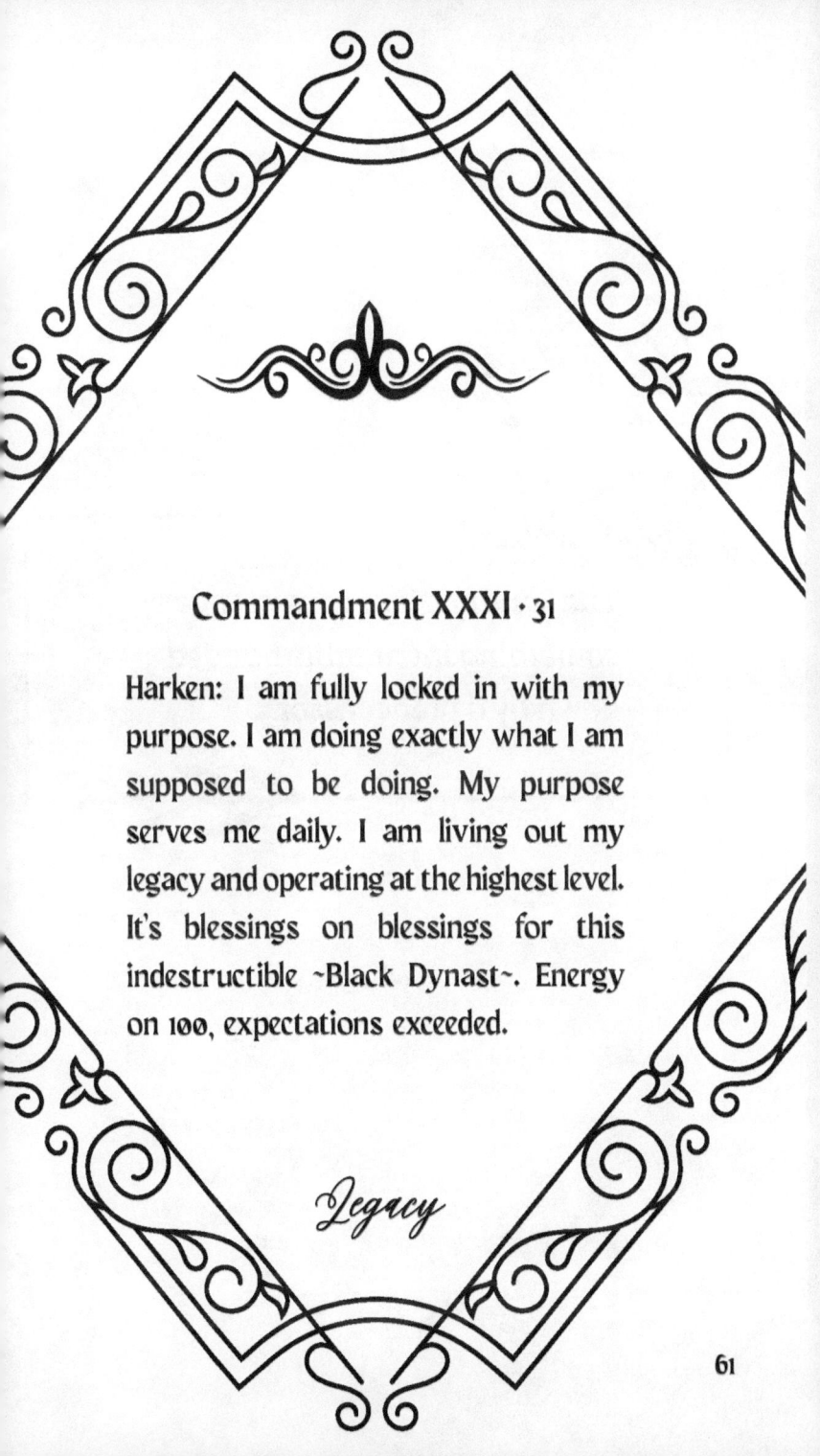

Commandment XXXI · 31

Harken: I am fully locked in with my purpose. I am doing exactly what I am supposed to be doing. My purpose serves me daily. I am living out my legacy and operating at the highest level. It's blessings on blessings for this indestructible ~Black Dynast~. Energy on 100, expectations exceeded.

Legacy

Legacy

The continuation or existence of something invaluable handed down by a predecessor.

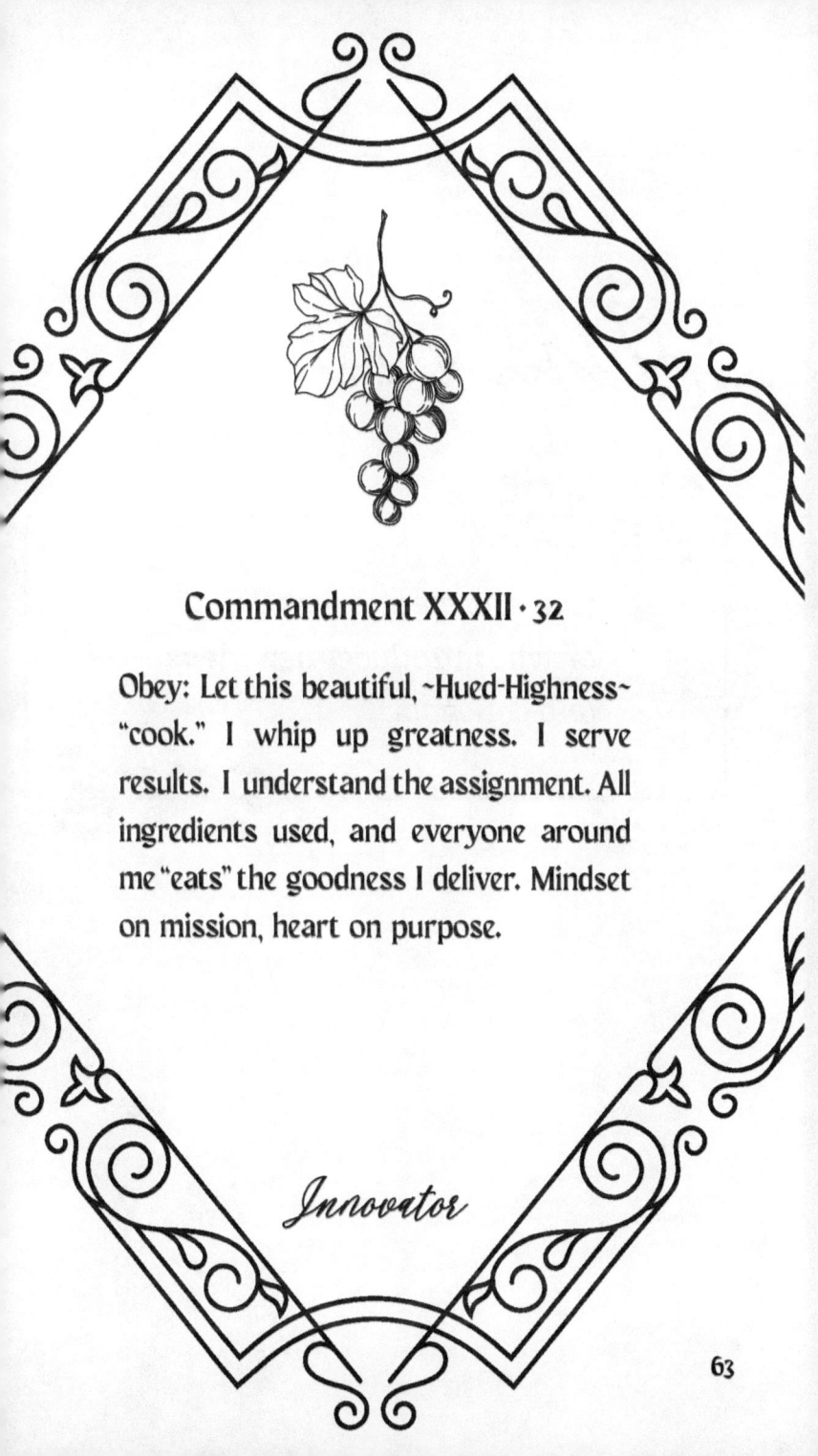

Commandment XXXII · 32

Obey: Let this beautiful, ~Hued-Highness~ "cook." I whip up greatness. I serve results. I understand the assignment. All ingredients used, and everyone around me "eats" the goodness I deliver. Mindset on mission, heart on purpose.

Innovator

Innovator

One who creates new things or who introduces new ideas and concepts.

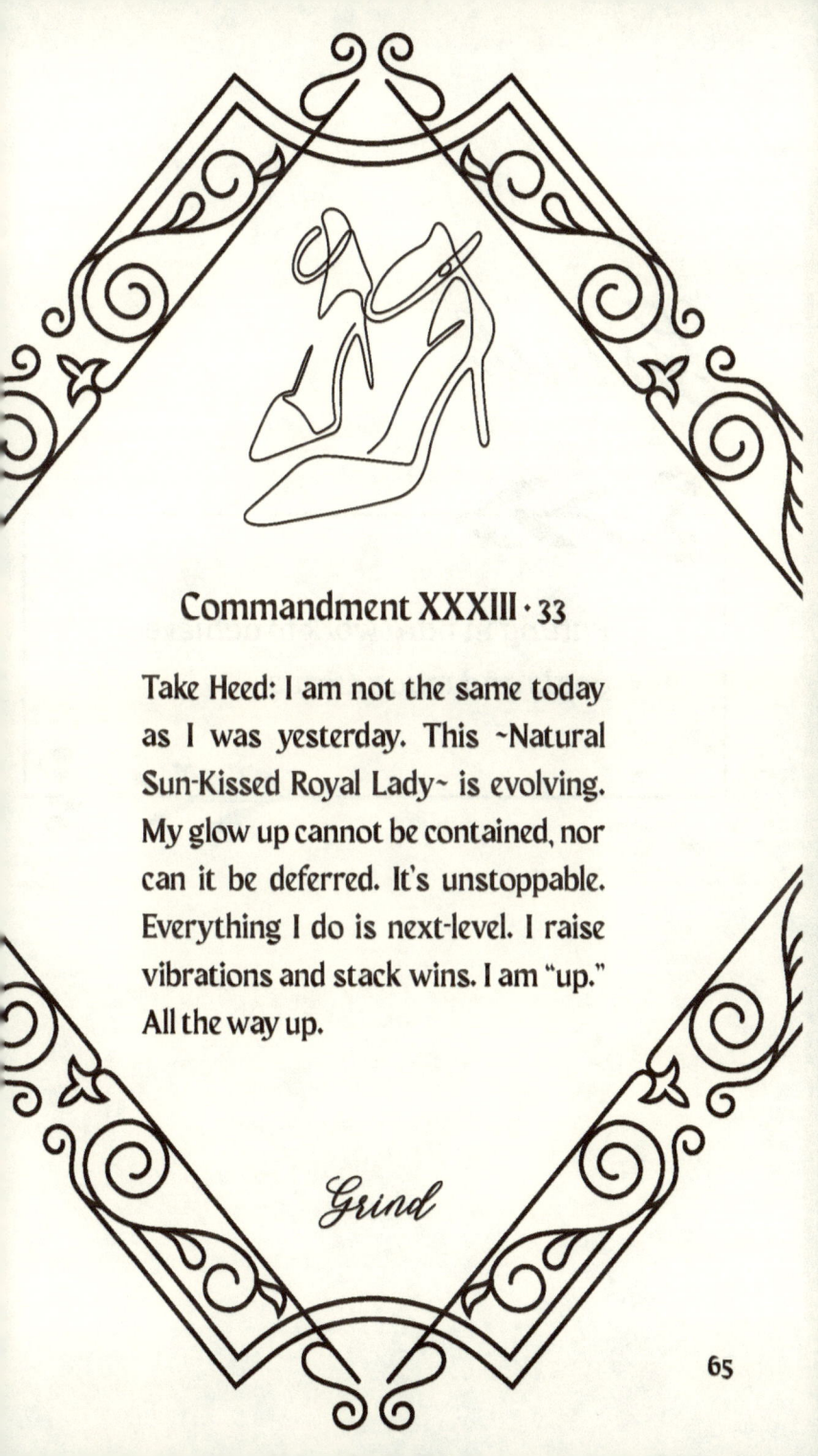

Commandment XXXIII · 33

Take Heed: I am not the same today as I was yesterday. This ~Natural Sun-Kissed Royal Lady~ is evolving. My glow up cannot be contained, nor can it be deferred. It's unstoppable. Everything I do is next-level. I raise vibrations and stack wins. I am "up." All the way up.

Grind

Grind

Putting in hard work to achieve
goals and reach status.

Commandment XXXIV · 34

Remember: I've got grit, grind, drive, and resilience. This ~Black-Bombshell Contessa~ does not take a backseat when it comes to securing the bag. I never give up. My eyes are always on the prize. This ~Black Queen~ always goes for the win. Don't play wit' it. Vision so clear, haters blurred.

Hustle

Hustle

Forcing and pushing through for progression.

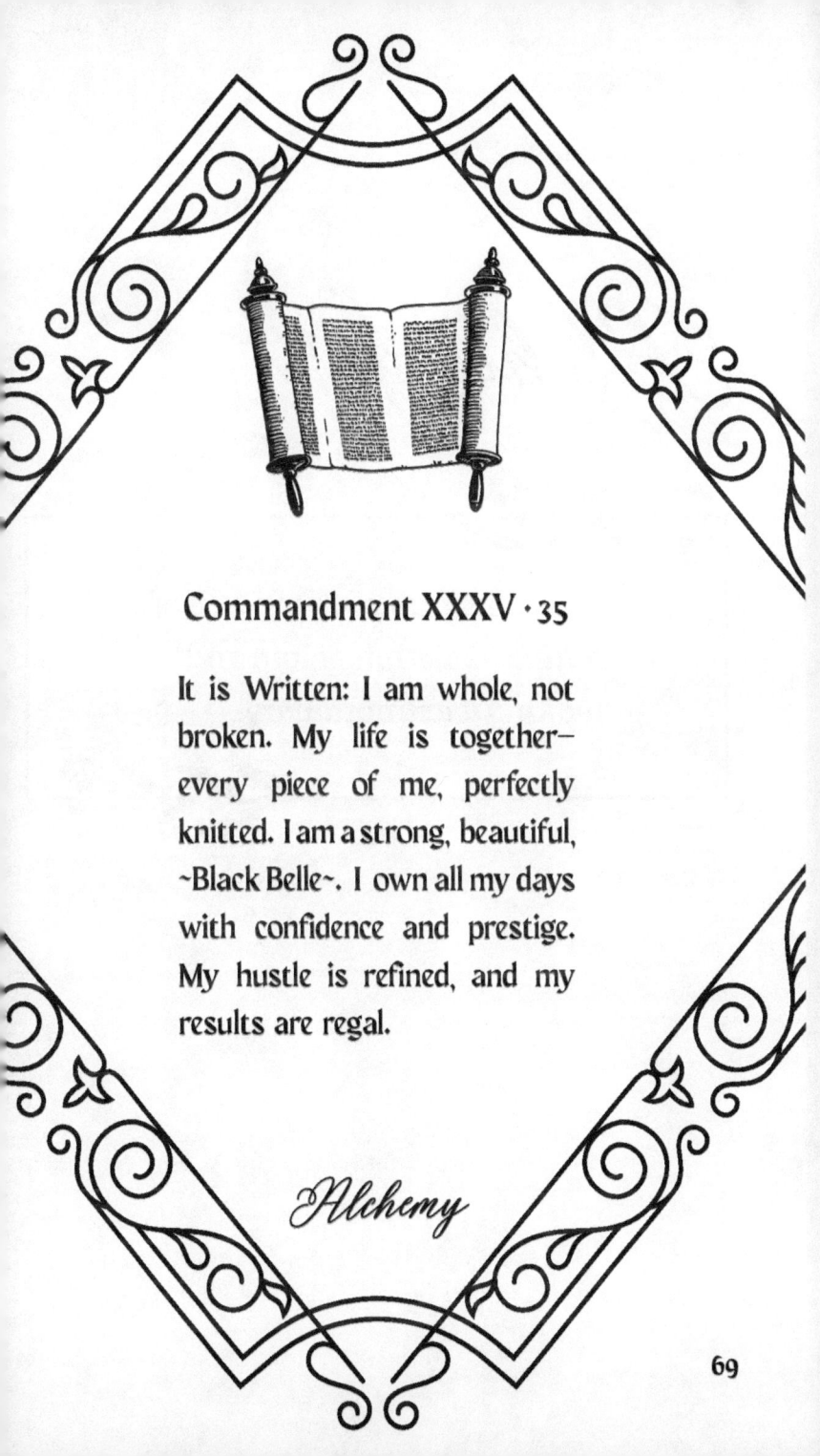

Commandment XXXV · 35

It is Written: I am whole, not broken. My life is together— every piece of me, perfectly knitted. I am a strong, beautiful, ~Black Belle~. I own all my days with confidence and prestige. My hustle is refined, and my results are regal.

Alchemy

Alchemy

> The transformation process of taking something plain and making it extraordinary.

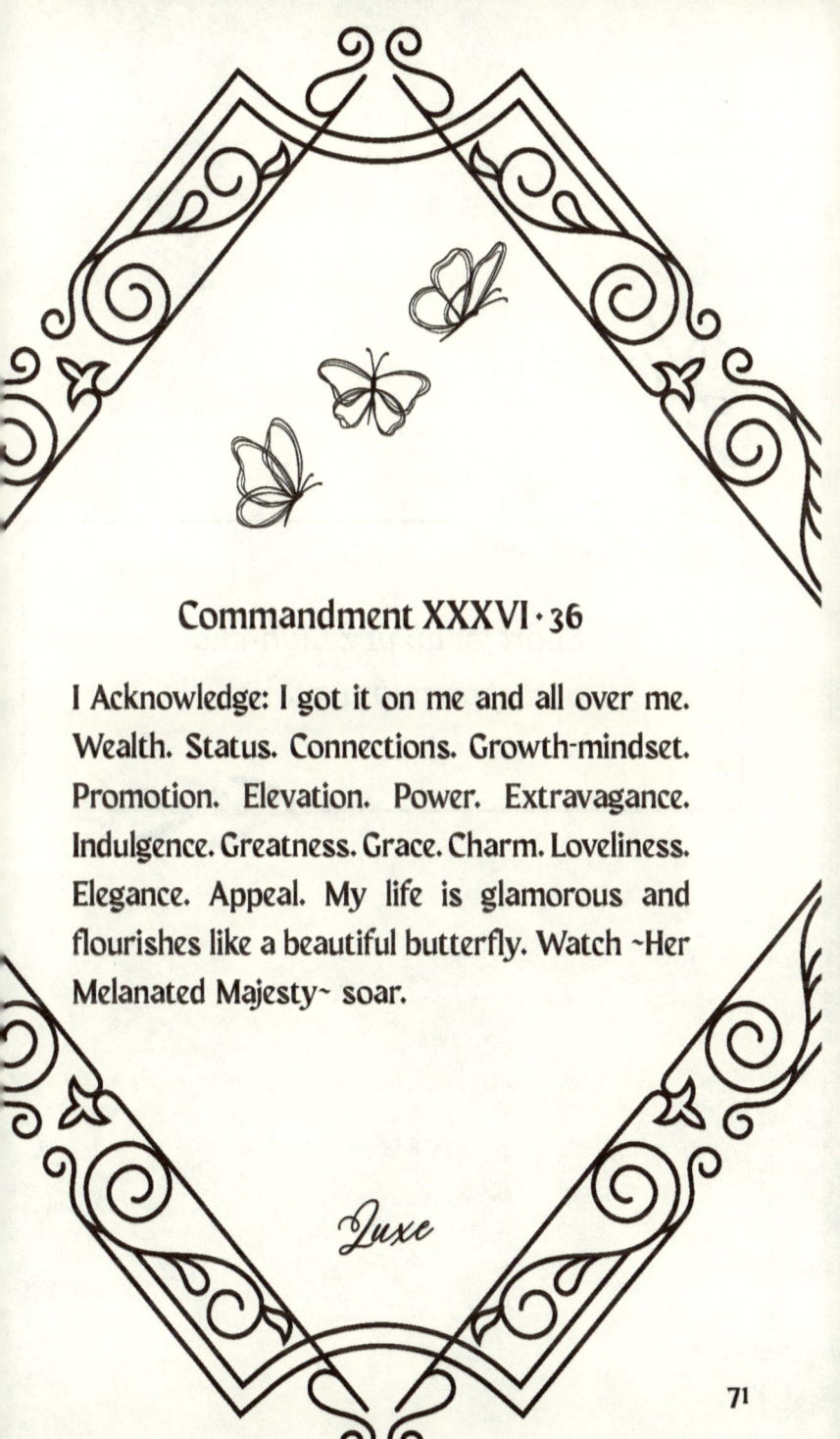

Commandment XXXVI · 36

I Acknowledge: I got it on me and all over me. Wealth. Status. Connections. Growth-mindset. Promotion. Elevation. Power. Extravagance. Indulgence. Greatness. Grace. Charm. Loveliness. Elegance. Appeal. My life is glamorous and flourishes like a beautiful butterfly. Watch ~Her Melanated Majesty~ soar.

Luxe

Luxe

Short for luxury, high-end
and of premium quality.

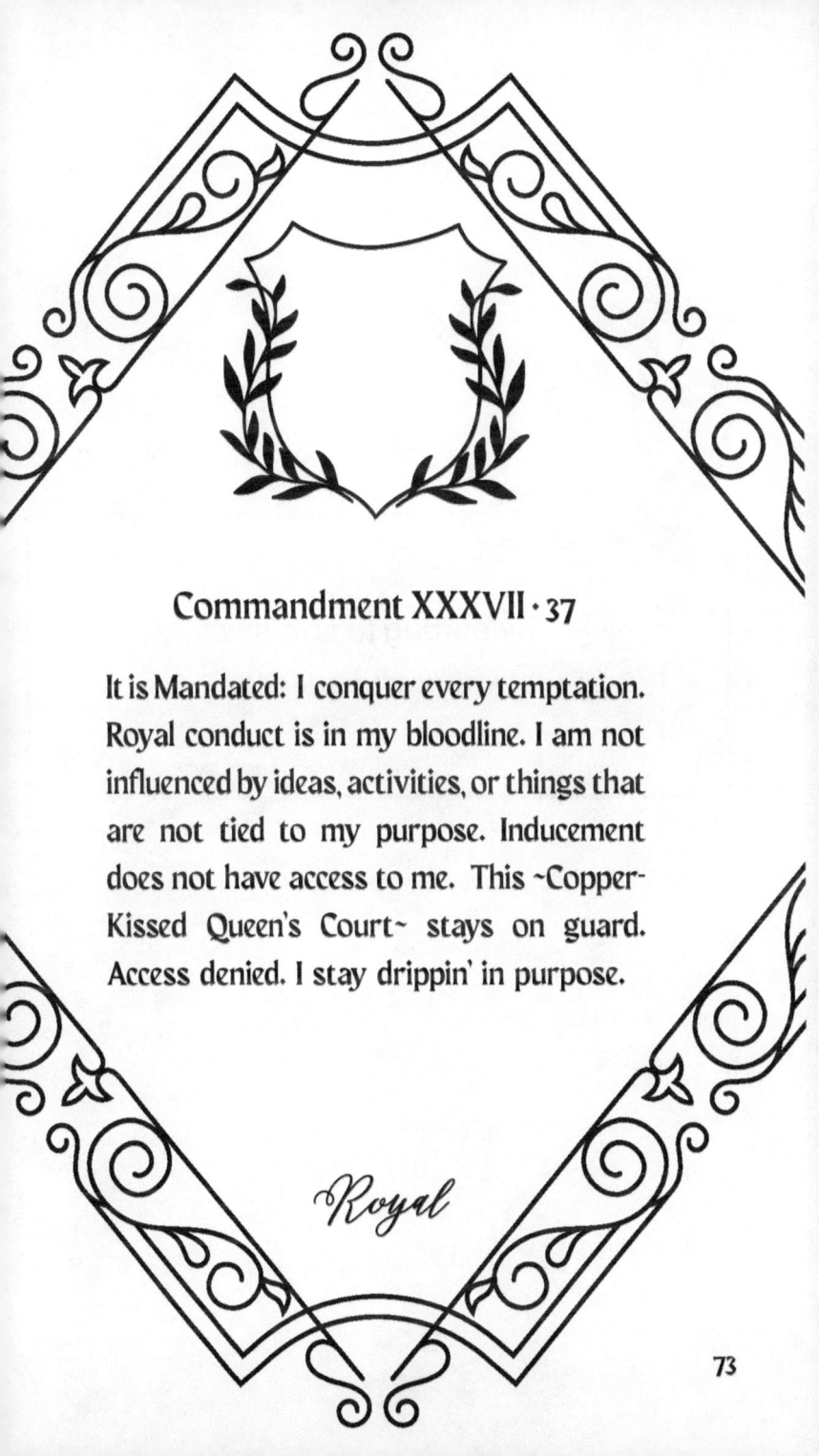

Commandment XXXVII · 37

It is Mandated: I conquer every temptation. Royal conduct is in my bloodline. I am not influenced by ideas, activities, or things that are not tied to my purpose. Inducement does not have access to me. This ~Copper-Kissed Queen's Court~ stays on guard. Access denied. I stay drippin' in purpose.

Royal

Royal

*Belonging to families
of kings and queens.*

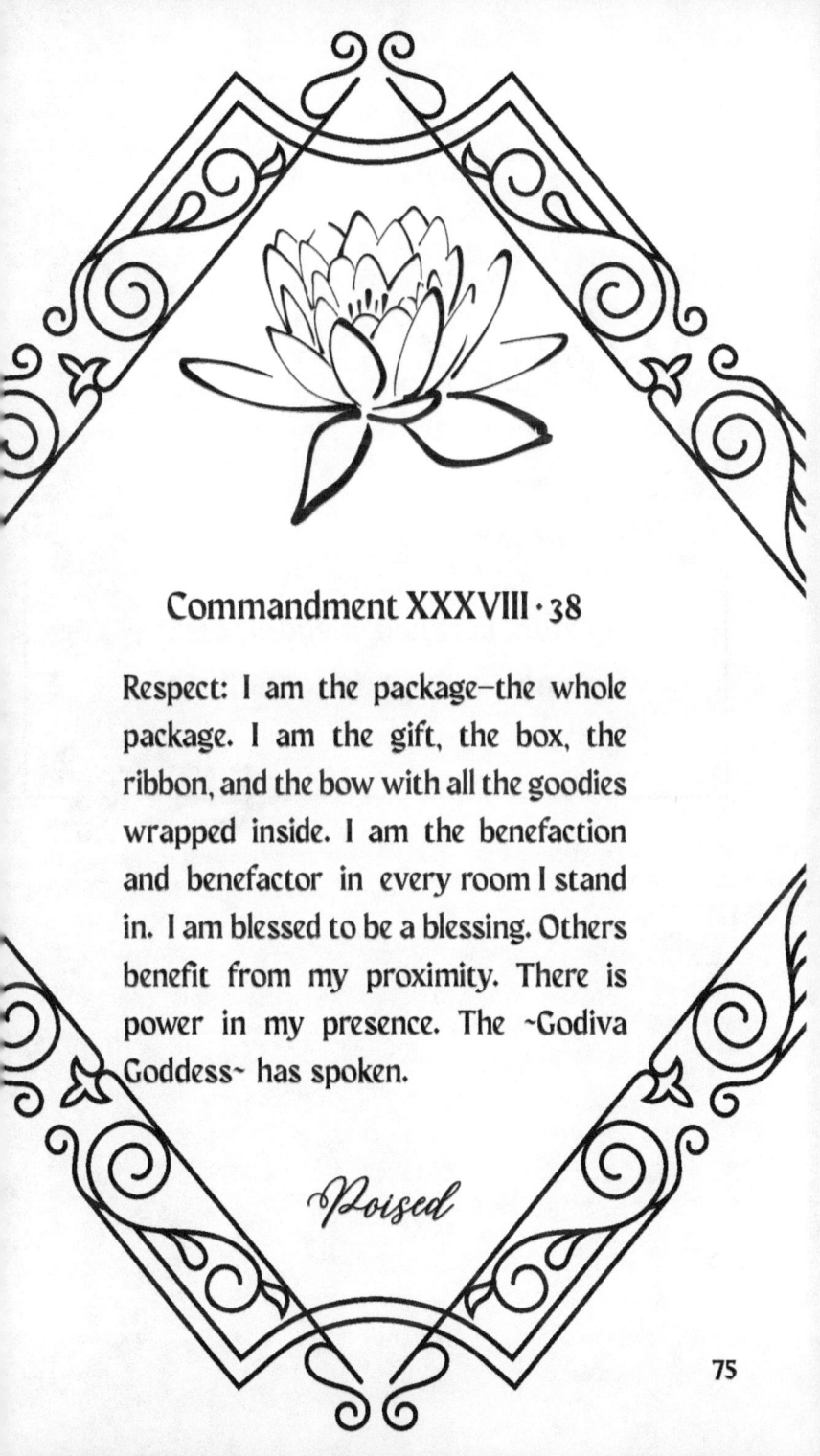

Commandment XXXVIII · 38

Respect: I am the package—the whole package. I am the gift, the box, the ribbon, and the bow with all the goodies wrapped inside. I am the benefaction and benefactor in every room I stand in. I am blessed to be a blessing. Others benefit from my proximity. There is power in my presence. The ~Godiva Goddess~ has spoken.

Poised

Poised

Calm, perched, elegant, and
ready to act or do something.

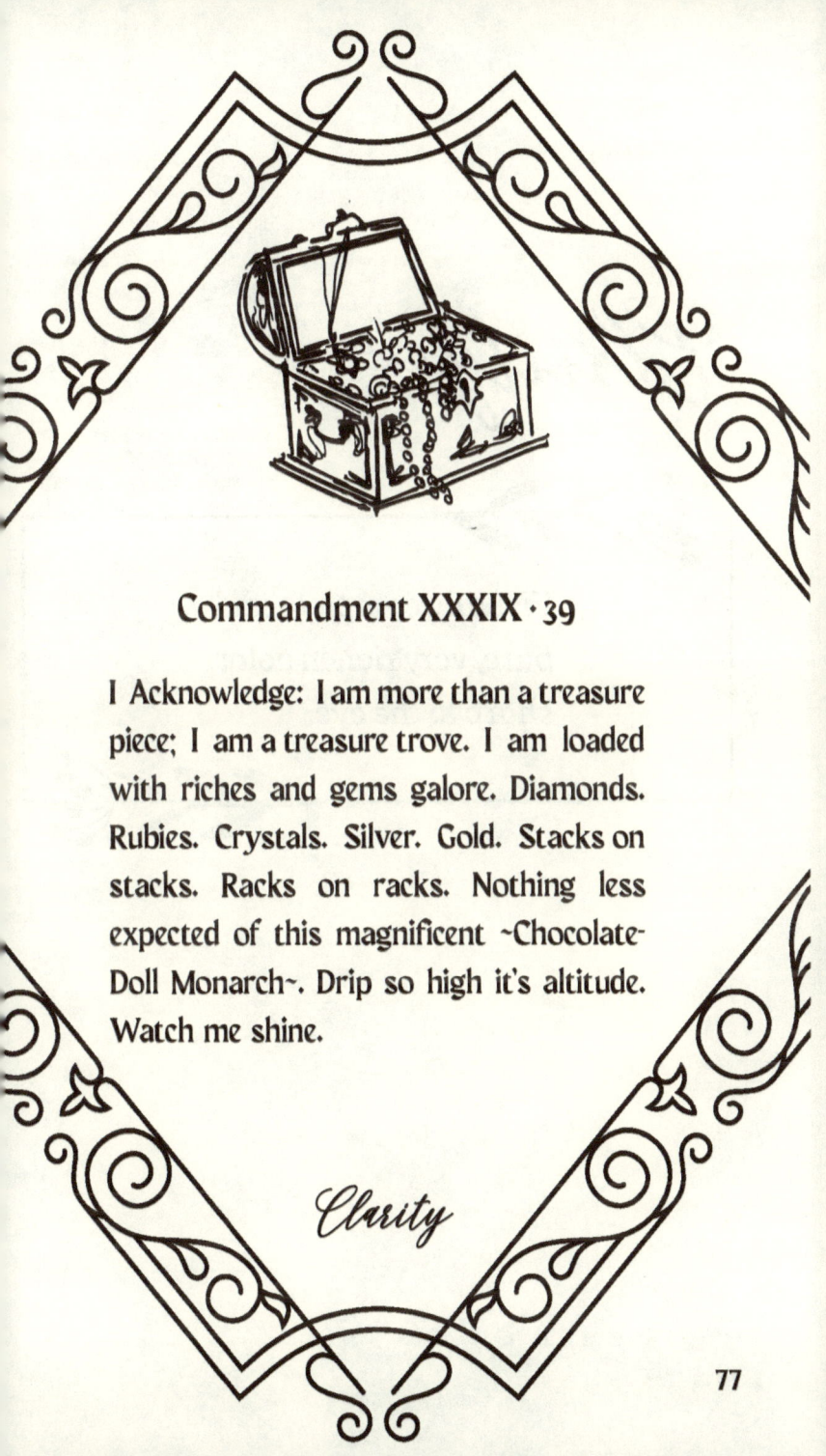

Commandment XXXIX · 39

I Acknowledge: I am more than a treasure piece; I am a treasure trove. I am loaded with riches and gems galore. Diamonds. Rubies. Crystals. Silver. Gold. Stacks on stacks. Racks on racks. Nothing less expected of this magnificent ~Chocolate-Doll Monarch~. Drip so high it's altitude. Watch me shine.

Clarity

Clarity

Visually complete and pure, very rich in color, sharp to the eye.

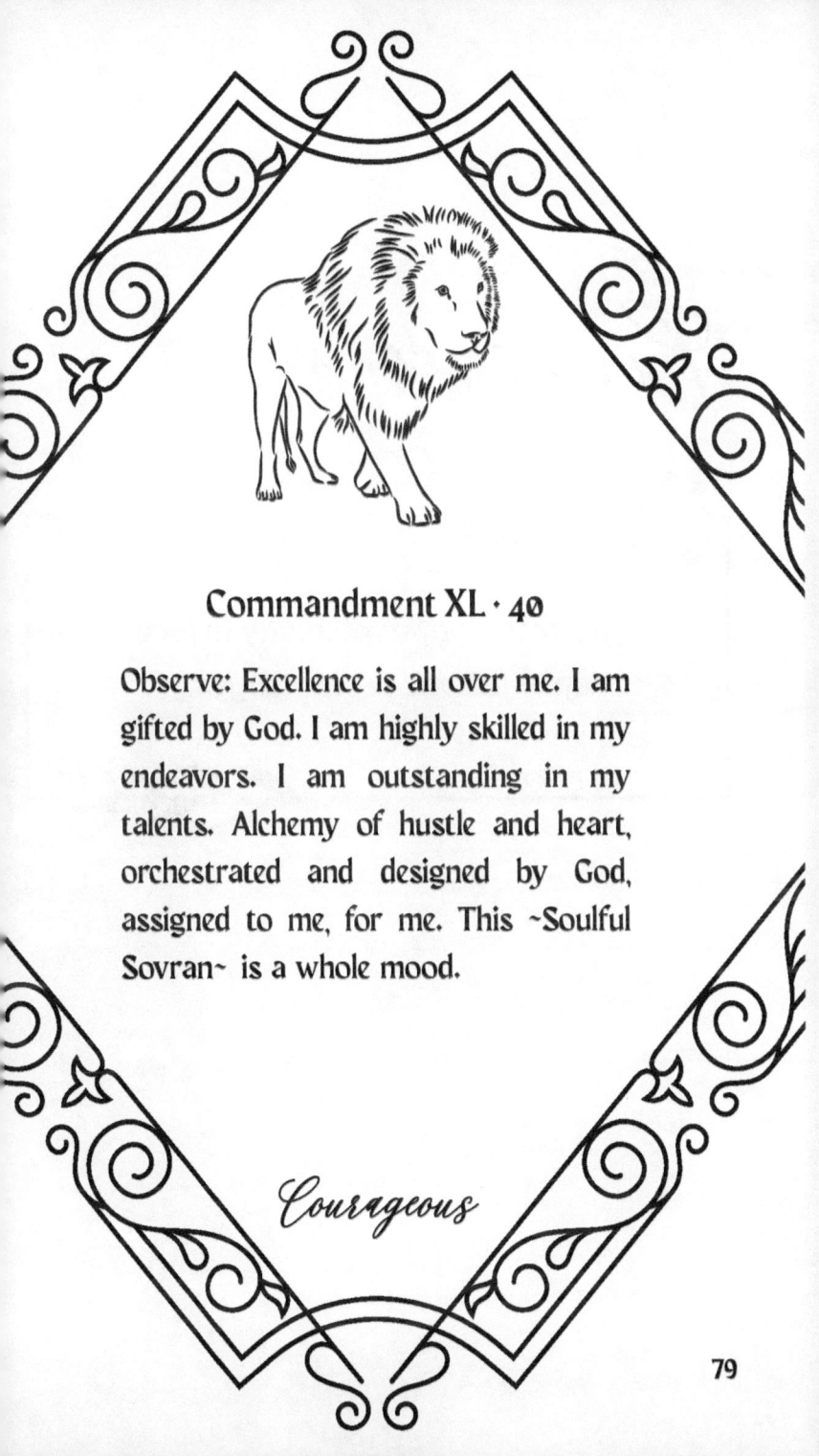

Commandment XL · 40

Observe: Excellence is all over me. I am gifted by God. I am highly skilled in my endeavors. I am outstanding in my talents. Alchemy of hustle and heart, orchestrated and designed by God, assigned to me, for me. This ~Soulful Sovran~ is a whole mood.

Courageous

Courageous

Fearless, confident, ready to face
confrontations or challenges.

Commandment XLI · 41

I Declare: My head is held high. Crown never tilted. This ~Ebony Epitome Empress~ parades her palace, affixed on the heavens above. My hue, glorious. My credence, affirmed. Quantum confidence unlocked. God is 100% on my side.

Ebony

Ebony

Deep, rich, black in color
and glorious beauty.

Commandment XLII · 42

Harken: I am a ~Hued Heroine~. I am a Leading Lady. I give Main Character Energy. I am a lovely, ~Dark-Tinted Demigoddess~. I put in the work and deliver the results effortlessly. I am a Superwoman. Others are baffled by how I get things done. I am victorious. I am inherently great and reign over my territory with all powers vested in me. Heavy on the elevation.

Regal

Regal

Dignified and impressive, suitable for royalty.

Commandment XLIII · 43

It is Abolished: No more tears. I no longer cry over those who break my heart. I no longer weep over my exes. I no longer wail over relationships or friendships that have ended. I no longer lament over things I cannot change. I no longer sob over my enemies. No more dwelling on the past. Gone are the crying days of this ~Coffee-Colored Chiefess~.

Powerhouse

Powerhouse

A force of strength determined to push through.

Commandment XLIV · 44

Observe: They might catch me slipping, but it will only be for a moment—and that's it. My comeback is unmatched. My wholeness and peace are always quickly restored. They watch and learn from me. I stay teaching. Through the good and the bad, my influence is forevermore. Now catch that "high tea." Teacup in hand, pinky finger up. Watch me sip.

Influential

Influential

One's actions or ways that persuade the minds or behavior of others.

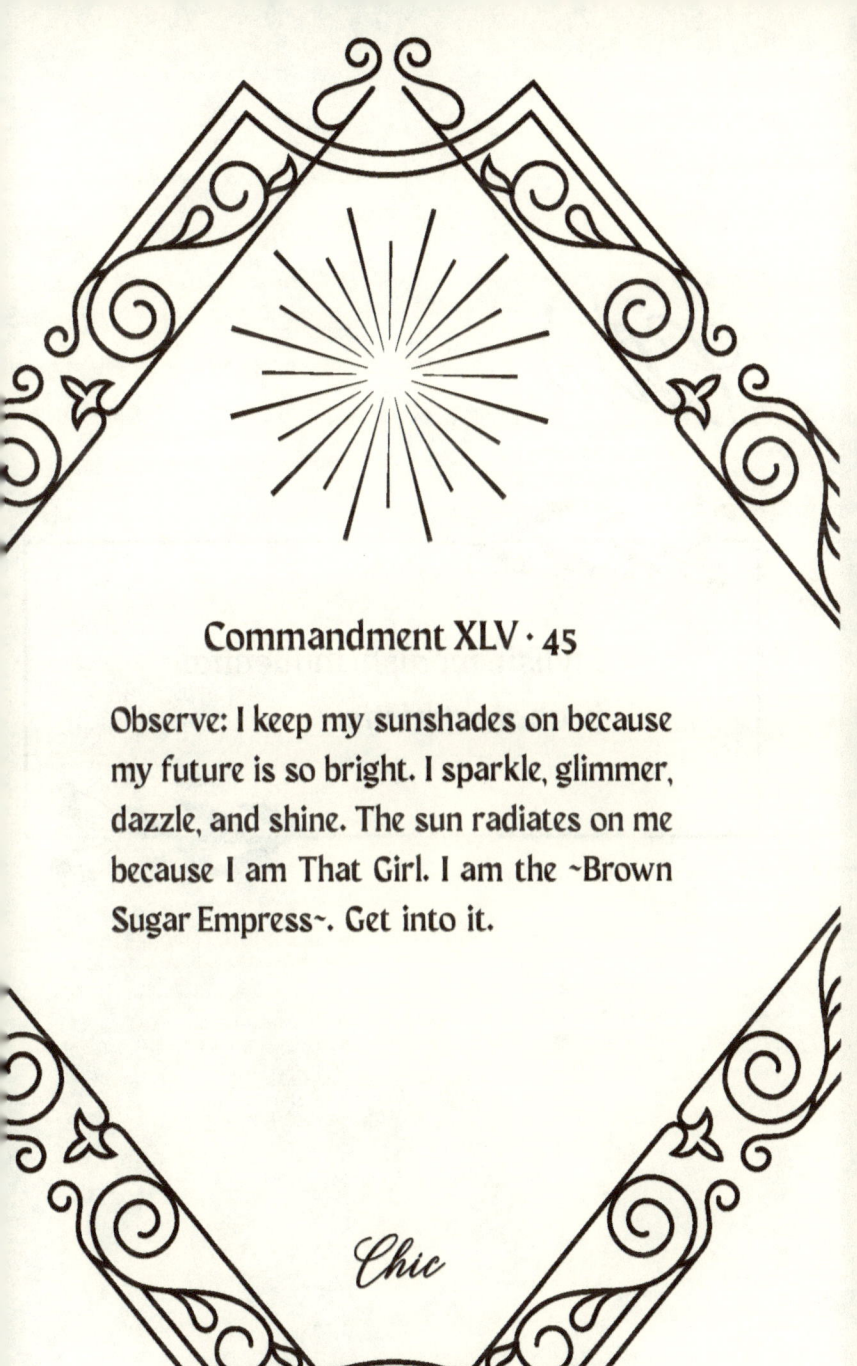

Commandment XLV · 45

Observe: I keep my sunshades on because my future is so bright. I sparkle, glimmer, dazzle, and shine. The sun radiates on me because I am That Girl. I am the ~Brown Sugar Empress~. Get into it.

Chic

Chic

> *Stylish, modish, influential in characteristic.*

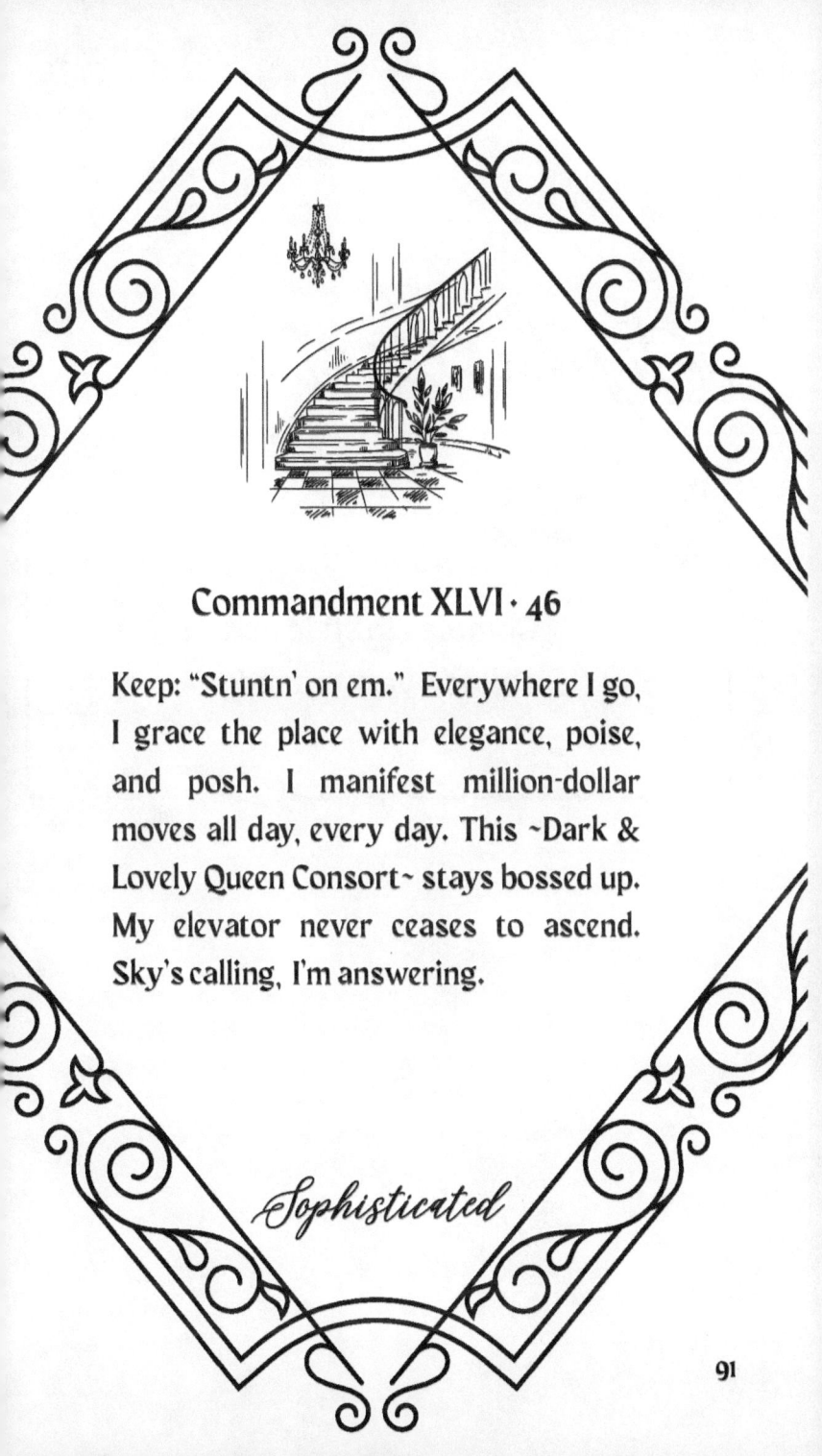

Commandment XLVI · 46

Keep: "Stuntn' on em." Everywhere I go, I grace the place with elegance, poise, and posh. I manifest million-dollar moves all day, every day. This ~Dark & Lovely Queen Consort~ stays bossed up. My elevator never ceases to ascend. Sky's calling, I'm answering.

Sophisticated

Sophisticated

Complex in style and
culture, very refined.

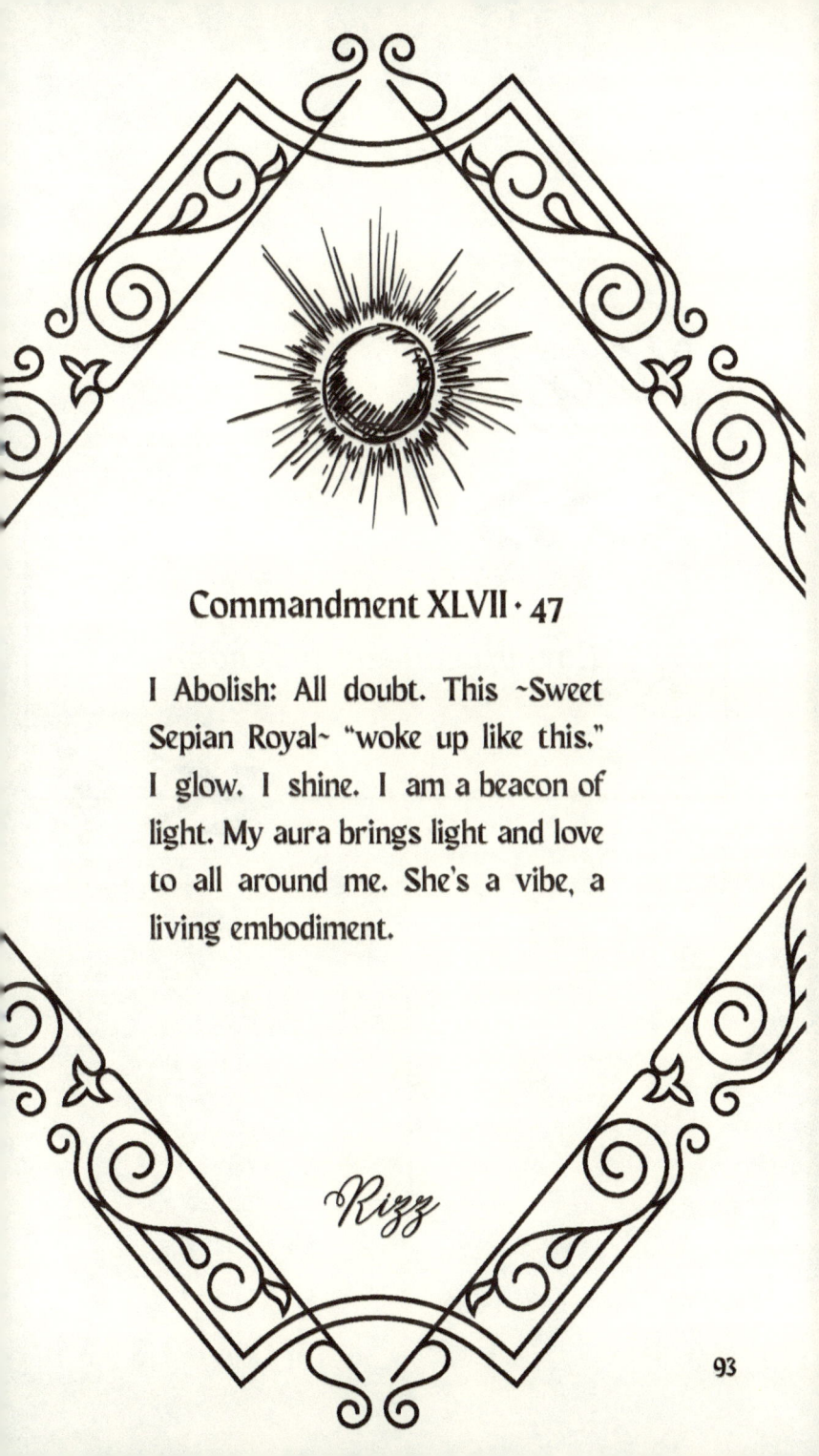

Commandment XLVII · 47

I Abolish: All doubt. This ~Sweet Sepian Royal~ "woke up like this." I glow. I shine. I am a beacon of light. My aura brings light and love to all around me. She's a vibe, a living embodiment.

Rizz

Rizz

Having charisma and charm.

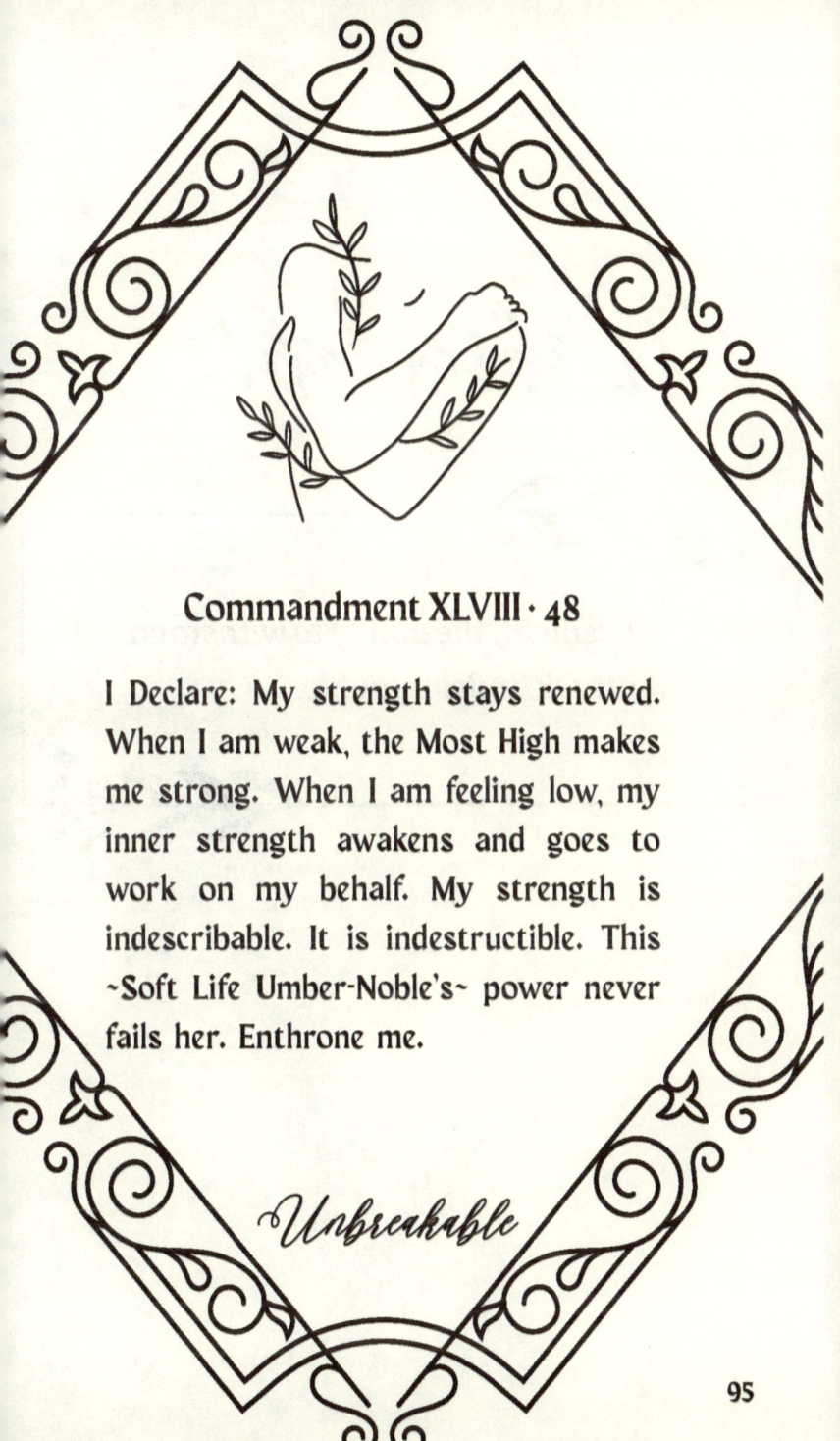

Commandment XLVIII · 48

I Declare: My strength stays renewed. When I am weak, the Most High makes me strong. When I am feeling low, my inner strength awakens and goes to work on my behalf. My strength is indescribable. It is indestructible. This ~Soft Life Umber-Noble's~ power never fails her. Enthrone me.

Unbreakable

Unbreakable

Resilient, the ability to withstand attack, indestructible.

Commandment XLIX · 49

Take Heed: There is no "I" in team, but there is a "me." When the team lets me down, I still have "me." Period.

Resurgence

Resurgence

A resurrection or comeback after experiencing downfall.

Commandment L · 50

Remember: Me, Myself, and I got this.
Momentum is in me. Drive is in me.
Purpose is in me. Determination is in
me. She's a walking affirmation.

Mindset

Mindset

The attitude and beliefs
that one holds.

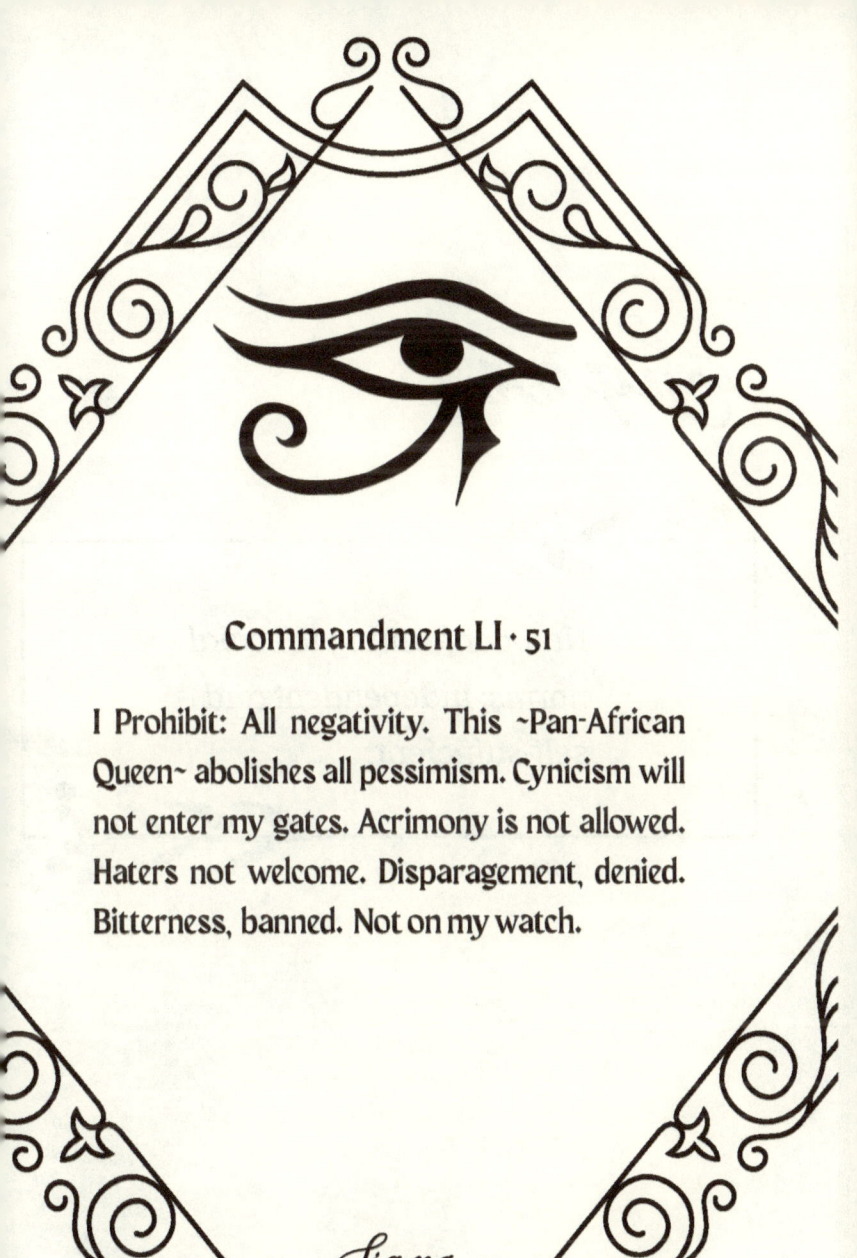

Commandment LI · 51

I Prohibit: All negativity. This ~Pan-African Queen~ abolishes all pessimism. Cynicism will not enter my gates. Acrimony is not allowed. Haters not welcome. Disparagement, denied. Bitterness, banned. Not on my watch.

Sigma

Sigma

Non-conforming to social norms; independent and self-sufficient.

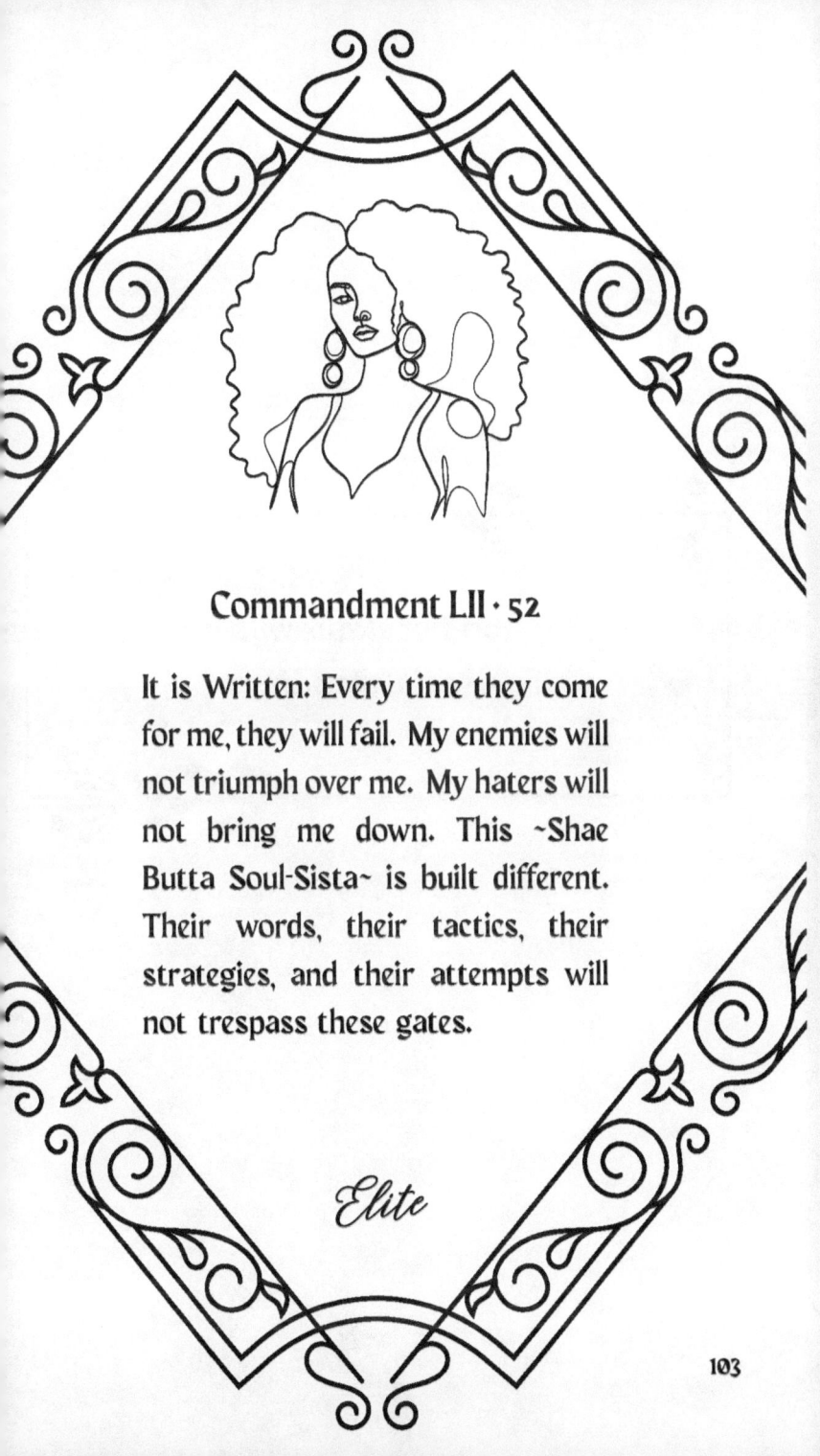

Commandment LII · 52

It is Written: Every time they come for me, they will fail. My enemies will not triumph over me. My haters will not bring me down. This ~Shae Butta Soul-Sista~ is built different. Their words, their tactics, their strategies, and their attempts will not trespass these gates.

Elite

Elite

*Of top-tier status with a
high social standing.*

Commandment LIII · 53

Attend: "I'm gon' be alright." This ~Copacetic Copper-Toned Majesty~ remains unbothered. No matter what I must face, I will conquer. I am victorious. It is decreed. I write the rules and follow them. ~Certified Queenie~.

Focused

Focused

Fully locked in on a specific goal without distractions.

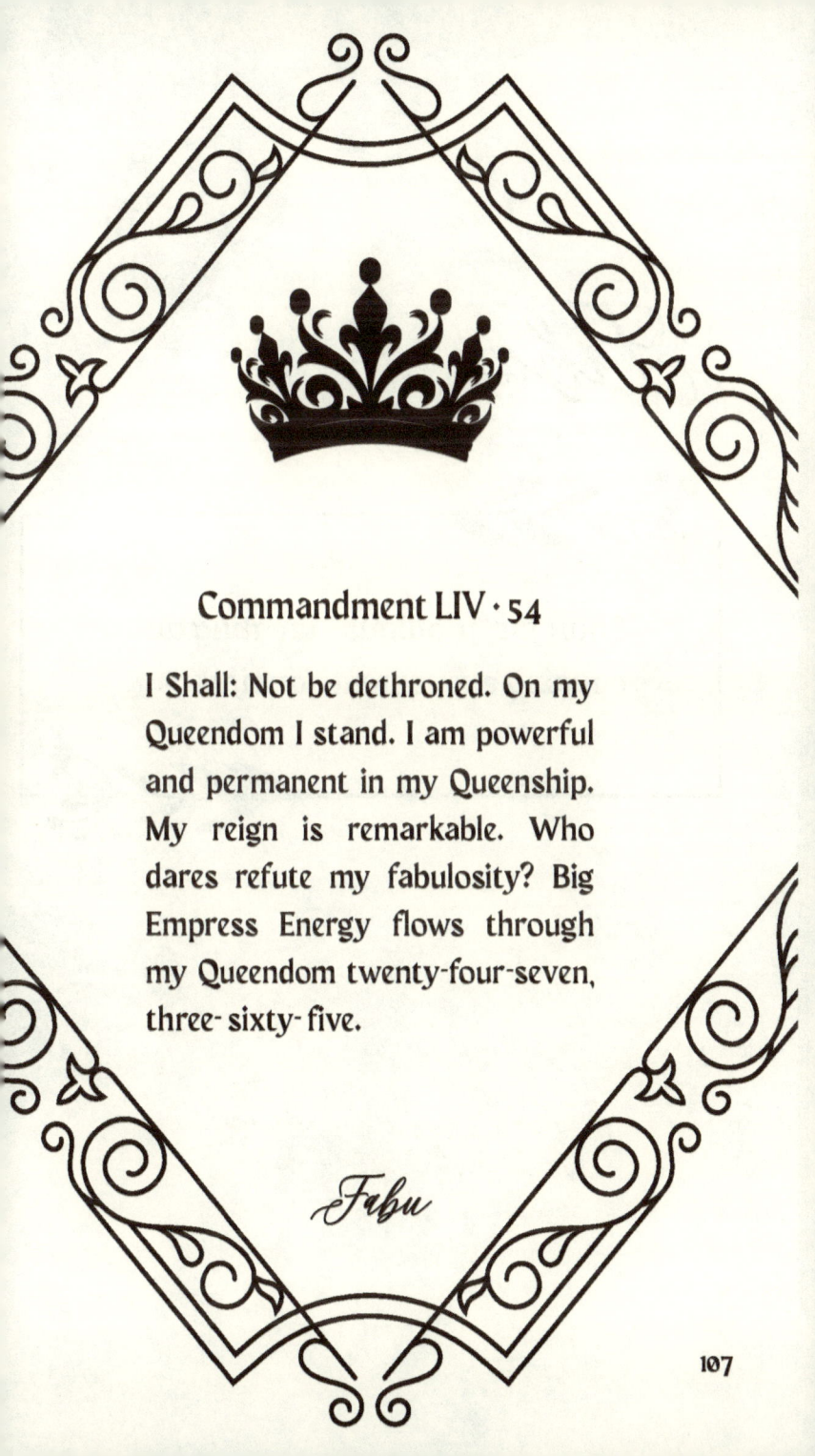

Commandment LIV · 54

I Shall: Not be dethroned. On my Queendom I stand. I am powerful and permanent in my Queenship. My reign is remarkable. Who dares refute my fabulosity? Big Empress Energy flows through my Queendom twenty-four-seven, three- sixty- five.

Fabu

Fabu

Short for "fabulous," creating and causing excitement, fanciful.

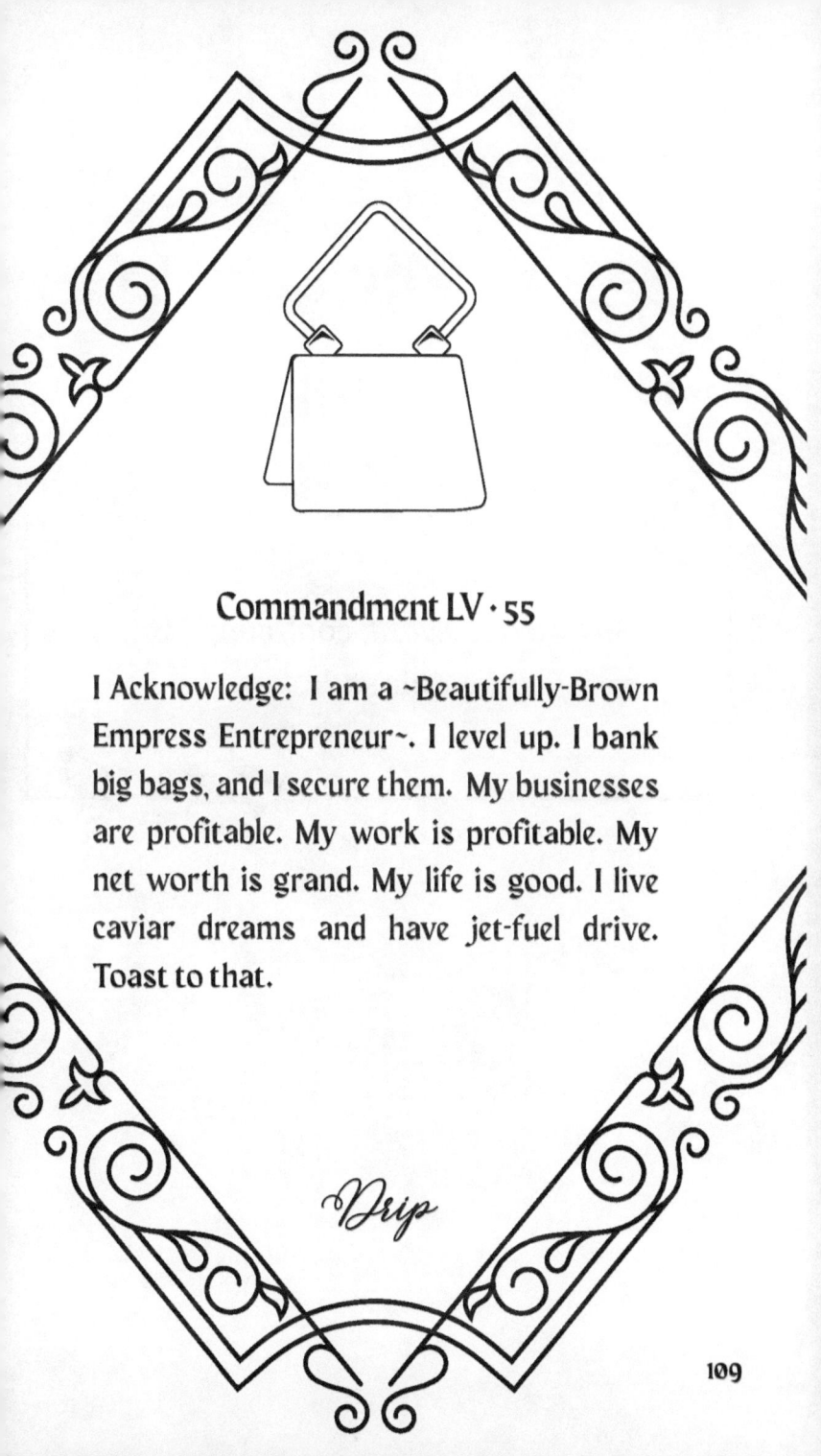

Commandment LV · 55

I Acknowledge: I am a ~Beautifully-Brown Empress Entrepreneur~. I level up. I bank big bags, and I secure them. My businesses are profitable. My work is profitable. My net worth is grand. My life is good. I live caviar dreams and have jet-fuel drive. Toast to that.

Drip

Drip

Having a relevant, cool, confident, and fashionable style.

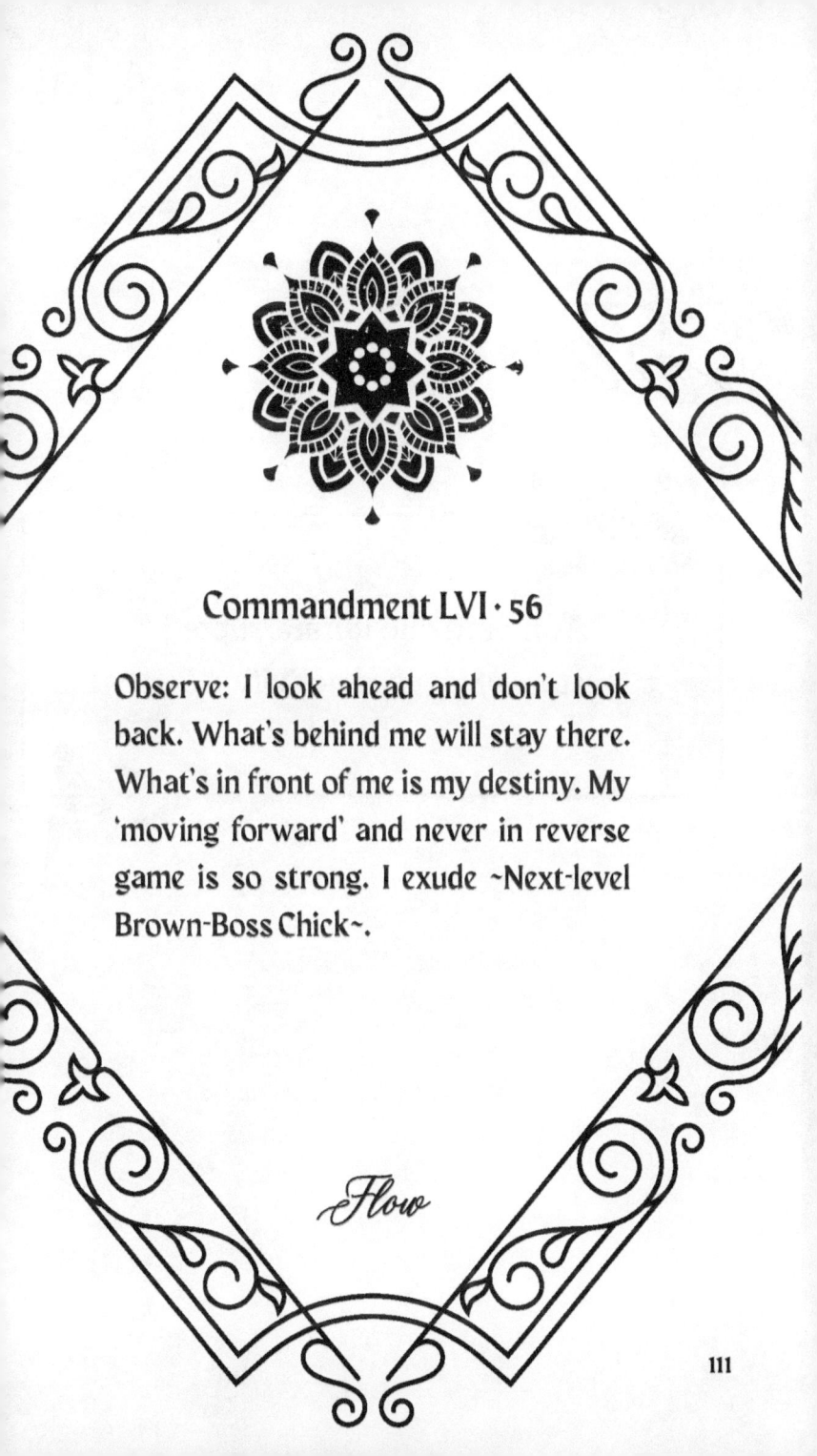

Commandment LVI · 56

Observe: I look ahead and don't look back. What's behind me will stay there. What's in front of me is my destiny. My 'moving forward' and never in reverse game is so strong. I exude ~Next-level Brown-Boss Chick~.

Flow

Flow

A smooth and uninterrupted
state of focused activity.

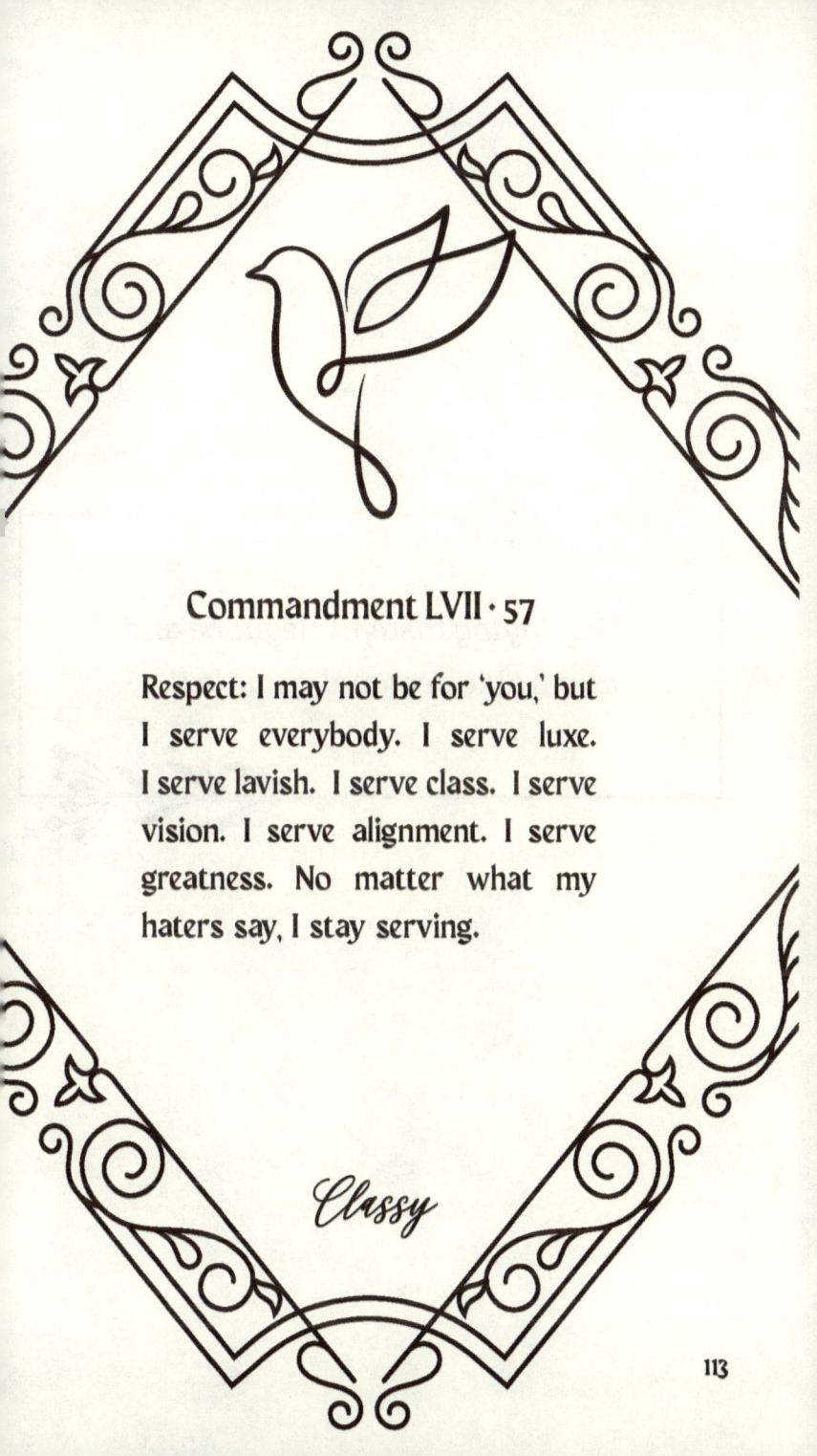

Commandment LVII · 57

Respect: I may not be for 'you,' but I serve everybody. I serve luxe. I serve lavish. I serve class. I serve vision. I serve alignment. I serve greatness. No matter what my haters say, I stay serving.

Classy

Classy

Displaying tasteful elegance and admirable personal qualities.

Commandment LVIII · 58

I Declare: My situations always work out for me. God's hands are upon this ~Precious Black Queen~. He fights my battles. I win every war. I am the King of Kings' daughter. Clock it.

Secured

Secured

Protected from hurt, harm, or danger, in a state of comfort and peace.

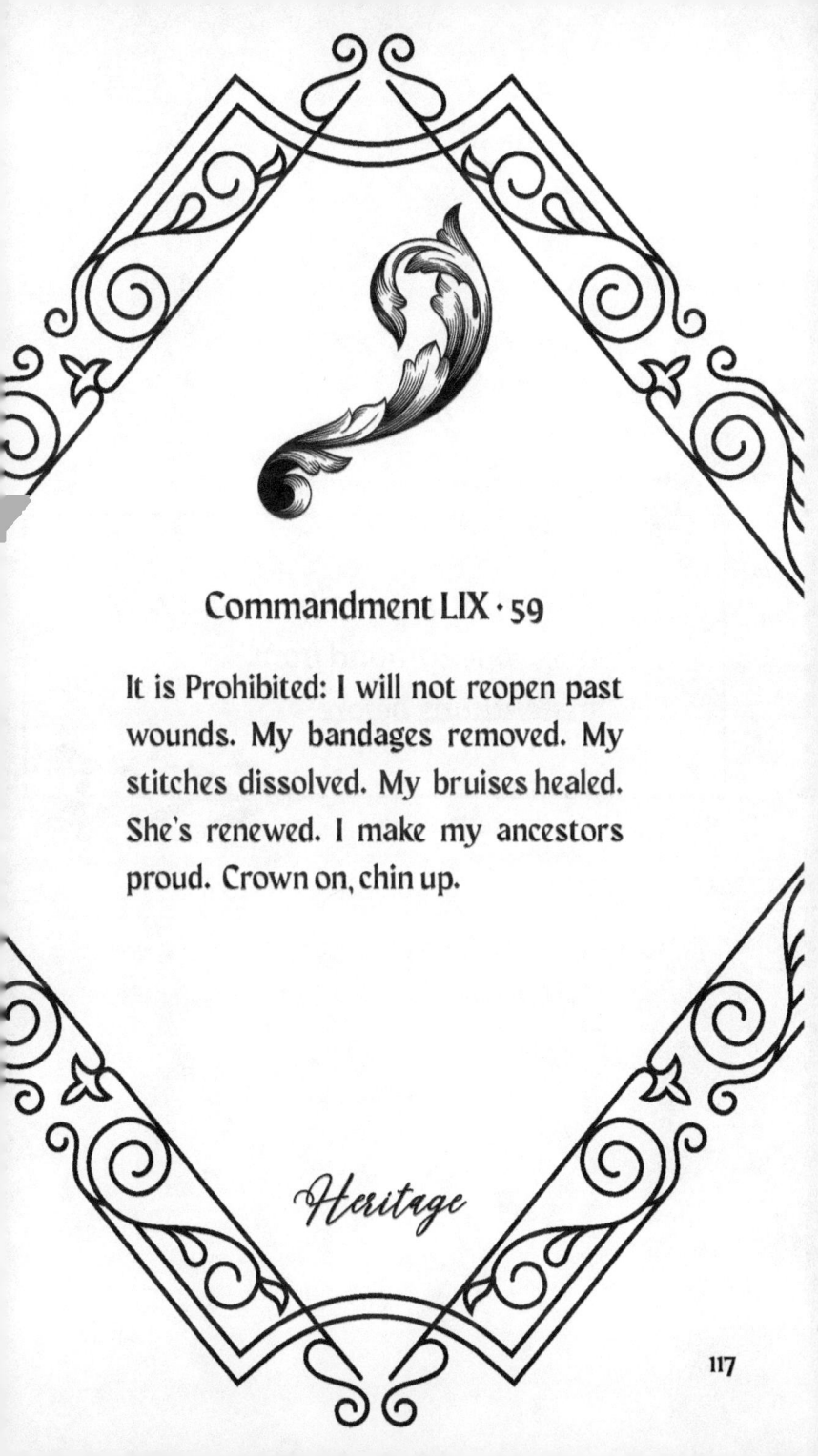

Commandment LIX · 59

It is Prohibited: I will not reopen past wounds. My bandages removed. My stitches dissolved. My bruises healed. She's renewed. I make my ancestors proud. Crown on, chin up.

Heritage

Heritage

Ancestral or inherited history,
one's background from
generations before.

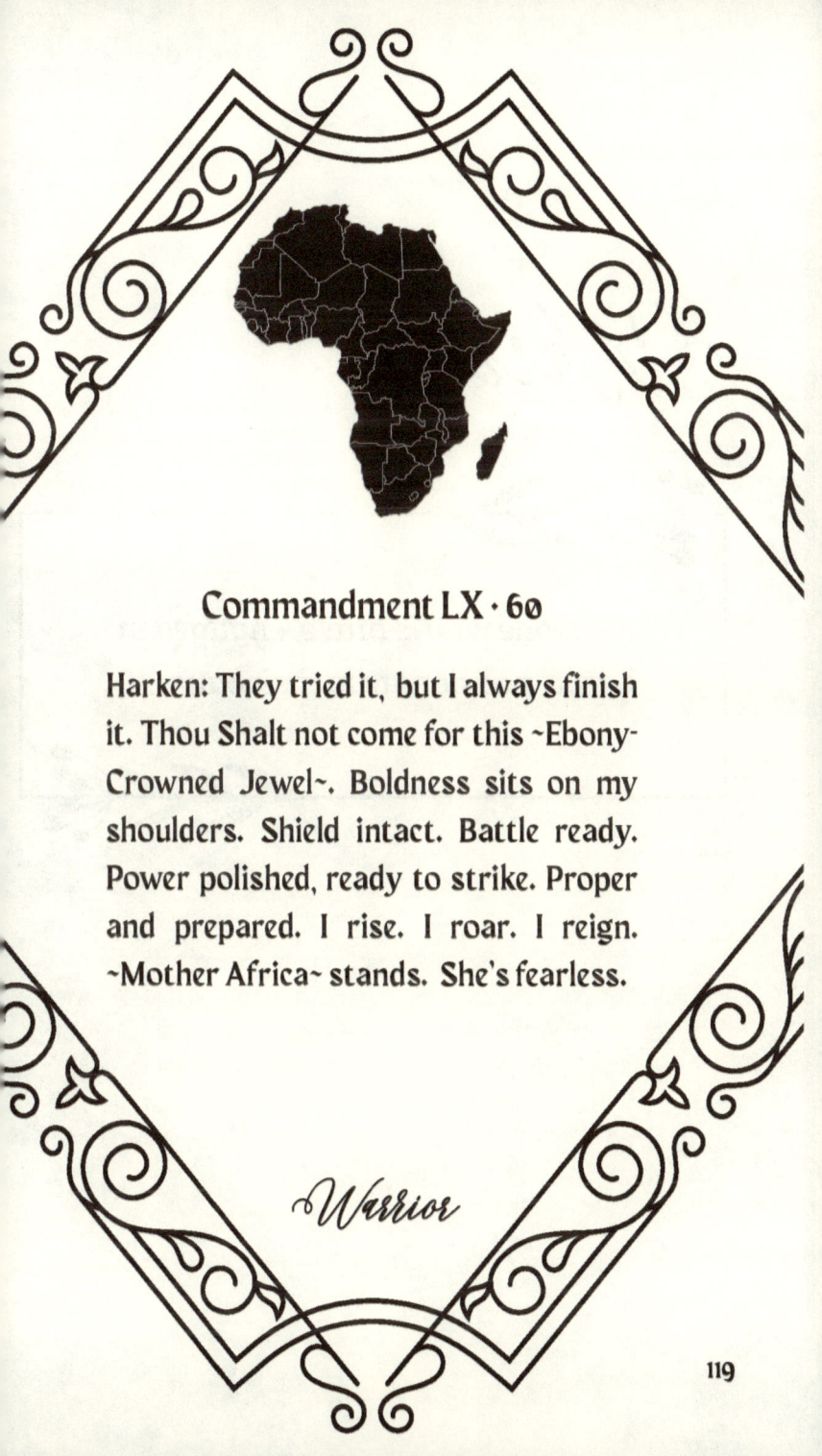

Commandment LX · 60

Harken: They tried it, but I always finish it. Thou Shalt not come for this ~Ebony-Crowned Jewel~. Boldness sits on my shoulders. Shield intact. Battle ready. Power polished, ready to strike. Proper and prepared. I rise. I roar. I reign. ~Mother Africa~ stands. She's fearless.

Warrior

Warrior

Someone who is brave, engaged in battle, passionate in their cause.

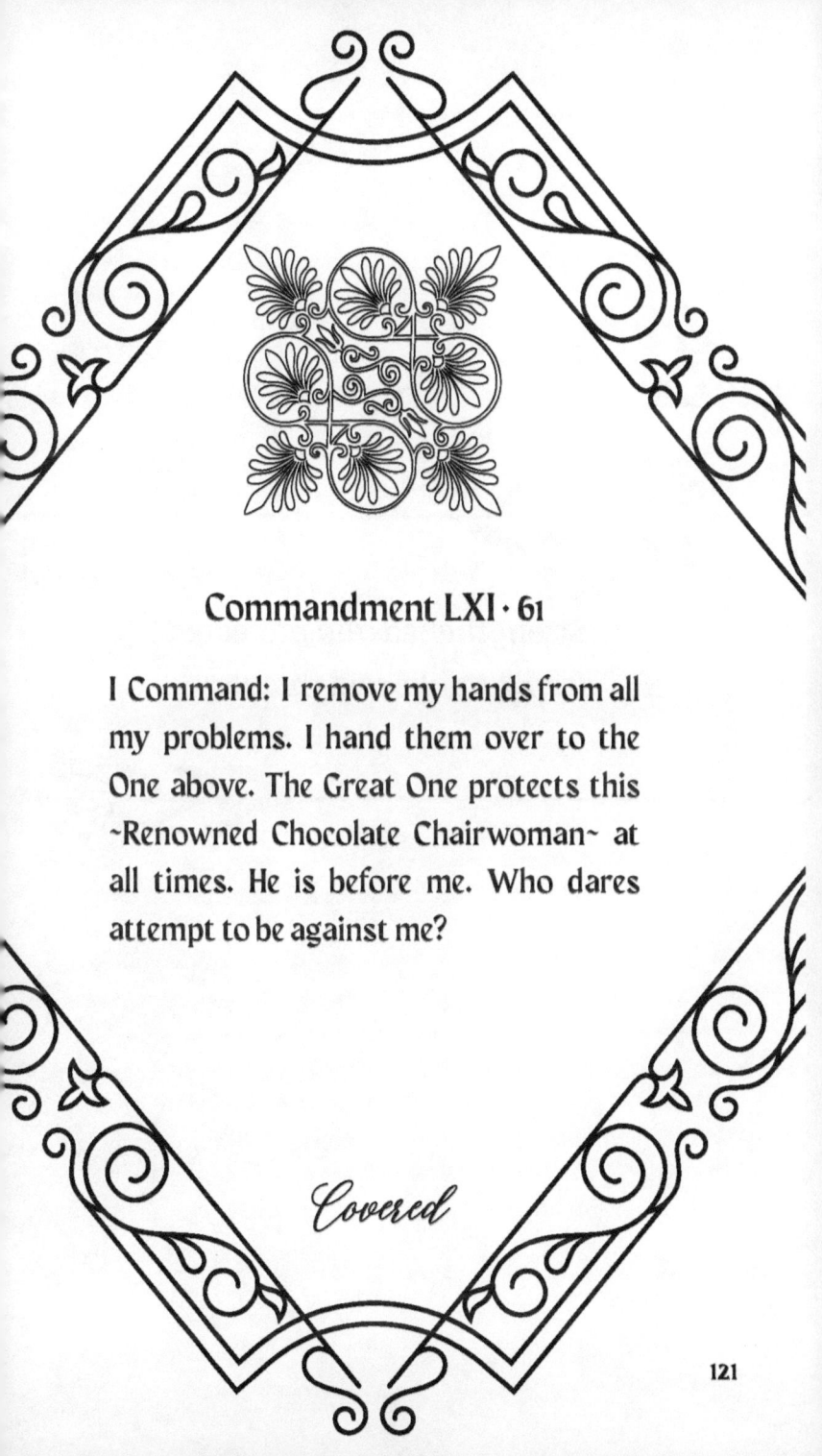

Commandment LXI · 61

I Command: I remove my hands from all my problems. I hand them over to the One above. The Great One protects this ~Renowned Chocolate Chairwoman~ at all times. He is before me. Who dares attempt to be against me?

Covered

Covered

> Strengthened and protected
> from attacks and threats.

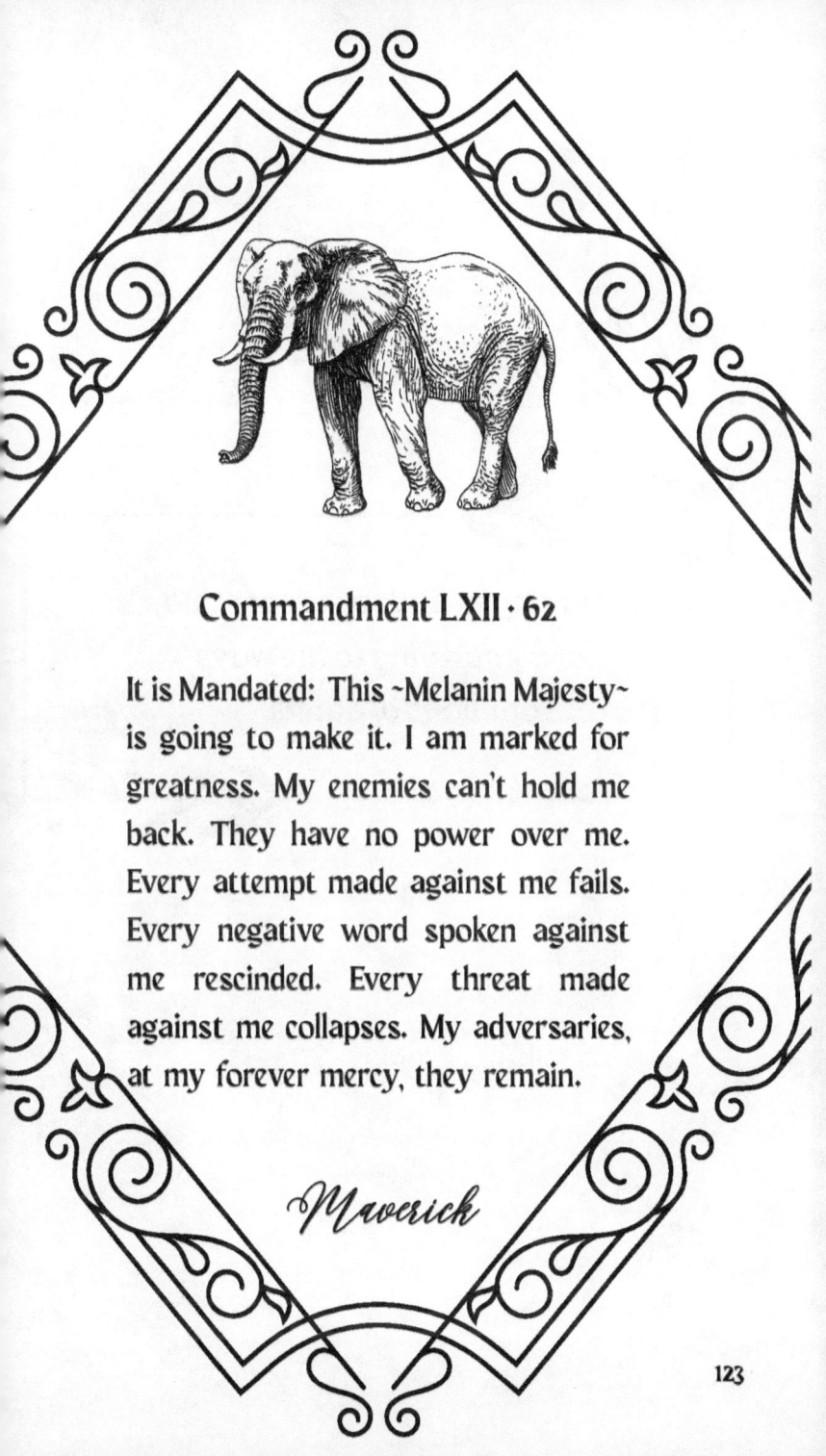

Commandment LXII · 62

It is Mandated: This ~Melanin Majesty~ is going to make it. I am marked for greatness. My enemies can't hold me back. They have no power over me. Every attempt made against me fails. Every negative word spoken against me rescinded. Every threat made against me collapses. My adversaries, at my forever mercy, they remain.

Maverick

Maverick

Having an independent mind,
not conforming to the ways
and opinions of others.

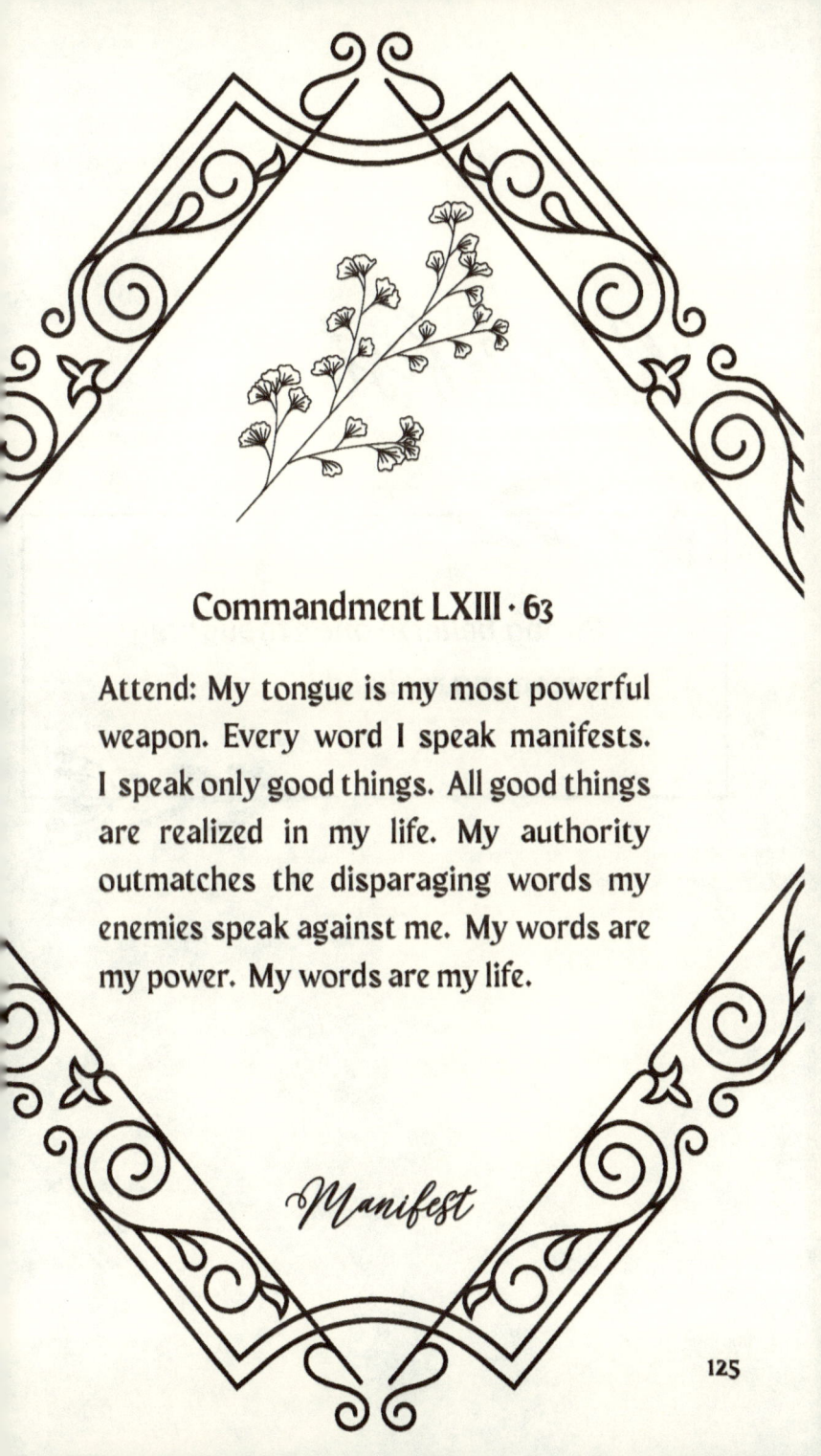

Commandment LXIII · 63

Attend: My tongue is my most powerful weapon. Every word I speak manifests. I speak only good things. All good things are realized in my life. My authority outmatches the disparaging words my enemies speak against me. My words are my power. My words are my life.

Manifest

Manifest

Strong belief in one's thoughts
becoming realized.

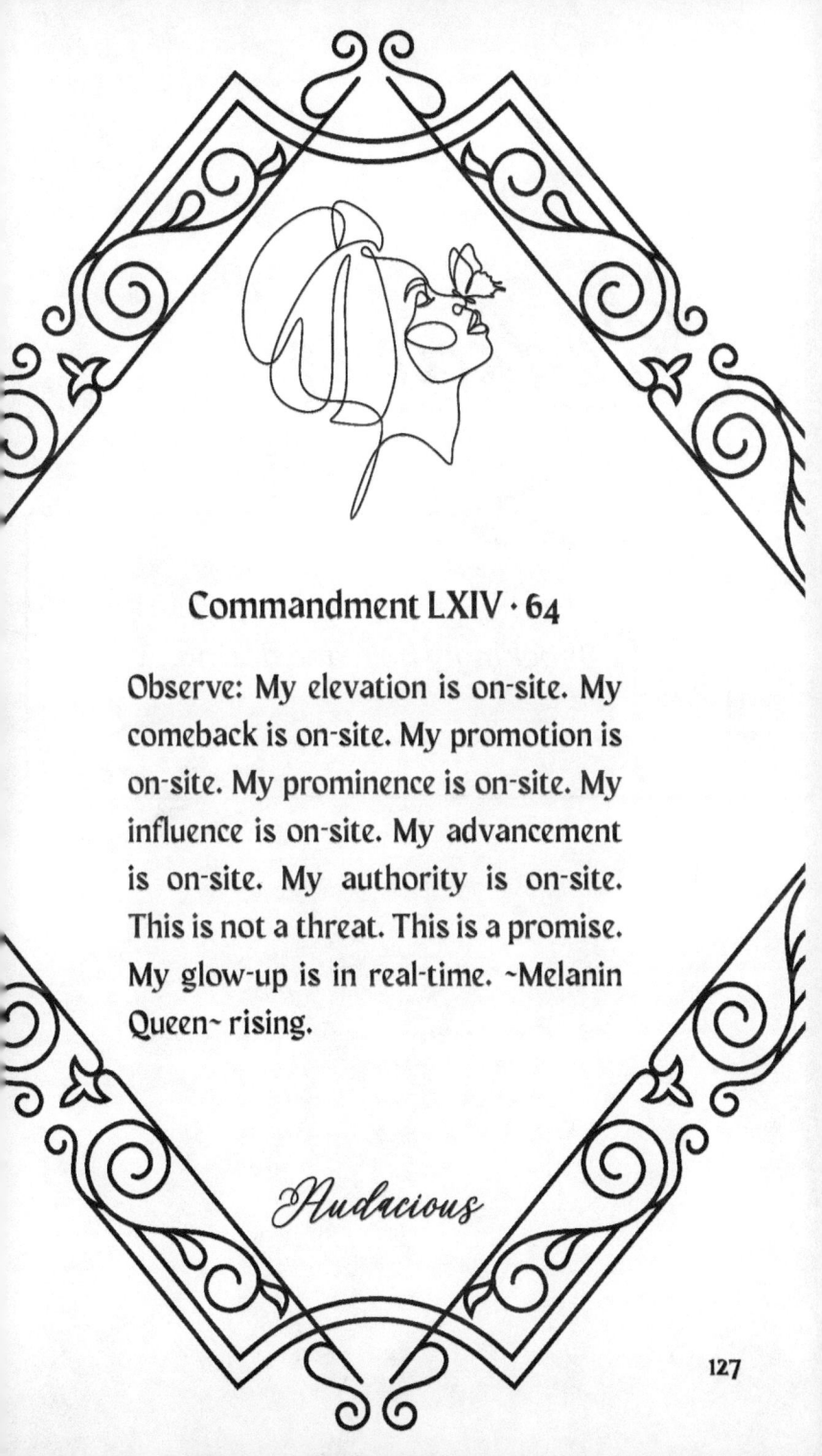

Commandment LXIV · 64

Observe: My elevation is on-site. My comeback is on-site. My promotion is on-site. My prominence is on-site. My influence is on-site. My advancement is on-site. My authority is on-site. This is not a threat. This is a promise. My glow-up is in real-time. ~Melanin Queen~ rising.

Audacious

Audacious

Shockingly bold and daring.

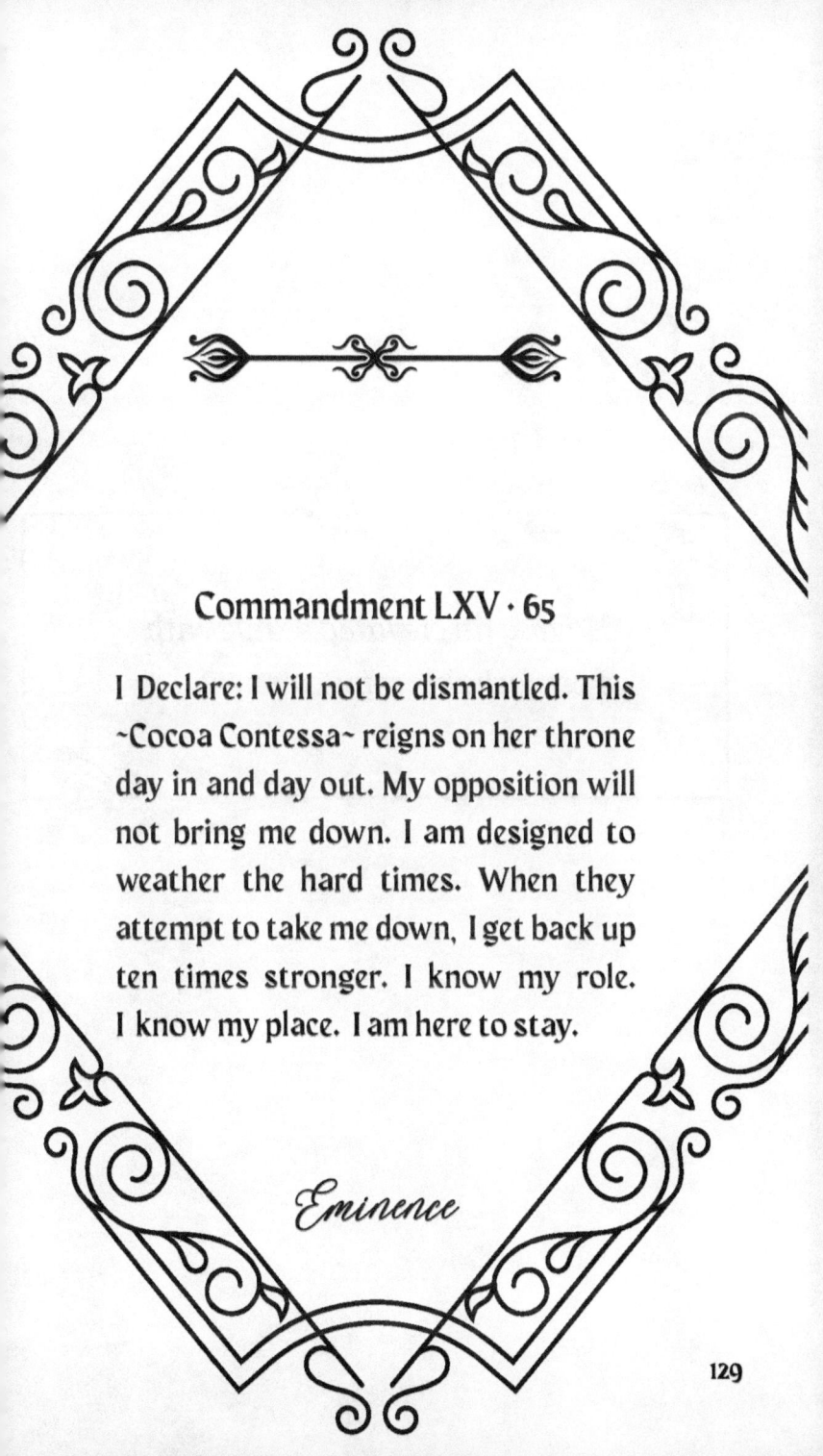

Commandment LXV · 65

I Declare: I will not be dismantled. This ~Cocoa Contessa~ reigns on her throne day in and day out. My opposition will not bring me down. I am designed to weather the hard times. When they attempt to take me down, I get back up ten times stronger. I know my role. I know my place. I am here to stay.

Eminence

Eminence

Having an elevated status with a remarkable reputation.

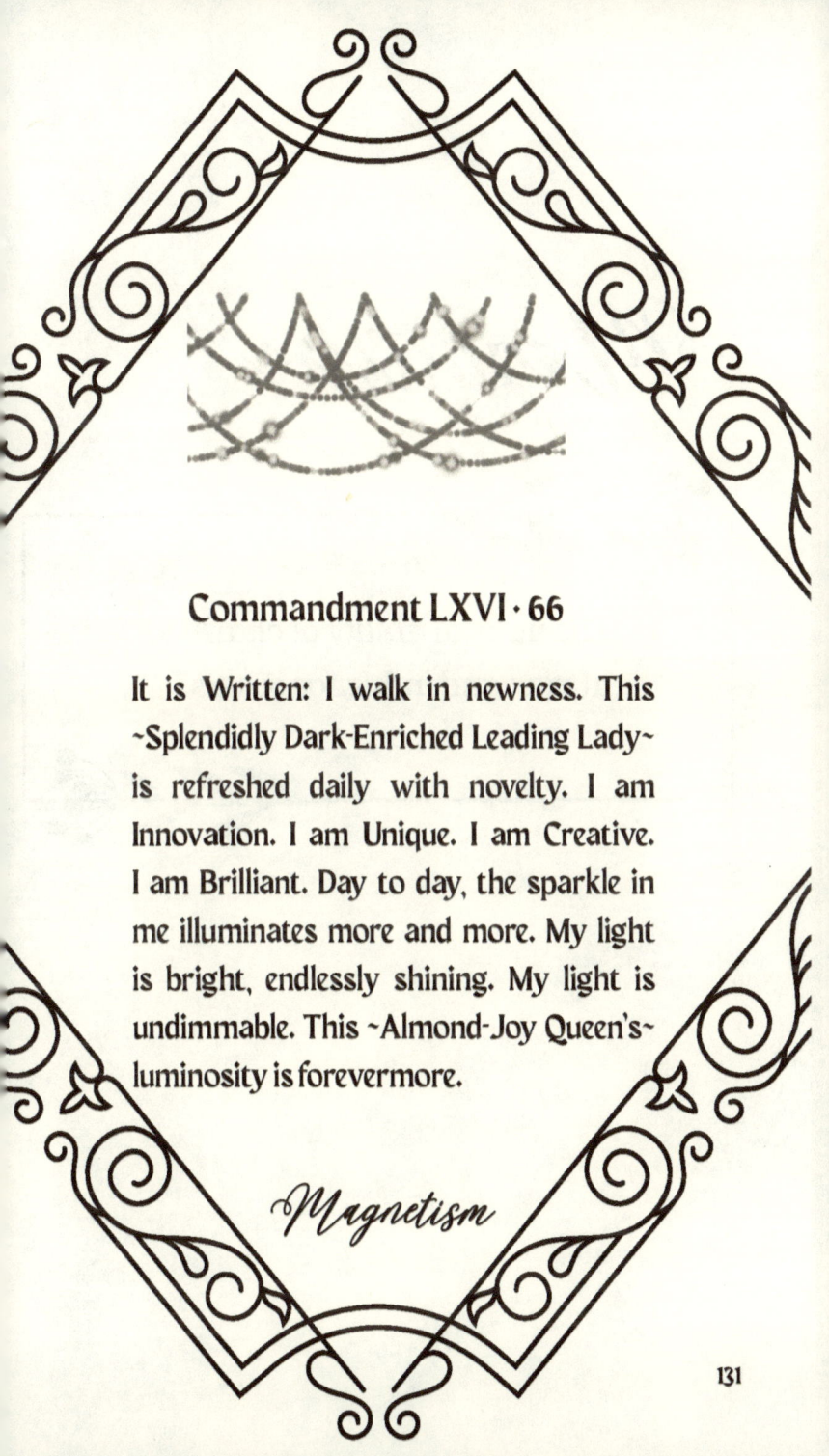

Commandment LXVI · 66

It is Written: I walk in newness. This
~Splendidly Dark-Enriched Leading Lady~
is refreshed daily with novelty. I am
Innovation. I am Unique. I am Creative.
I am Brilliant. Day to day, the sparkle in
me illuminates more and more. My light
is bright, endlessly shining. My light is
undimmable. This ~Almond-Joy Queen's~
luminosity is forevermore.

Magnetism

Magnetism

The natural ability or charm to attract and influence others.

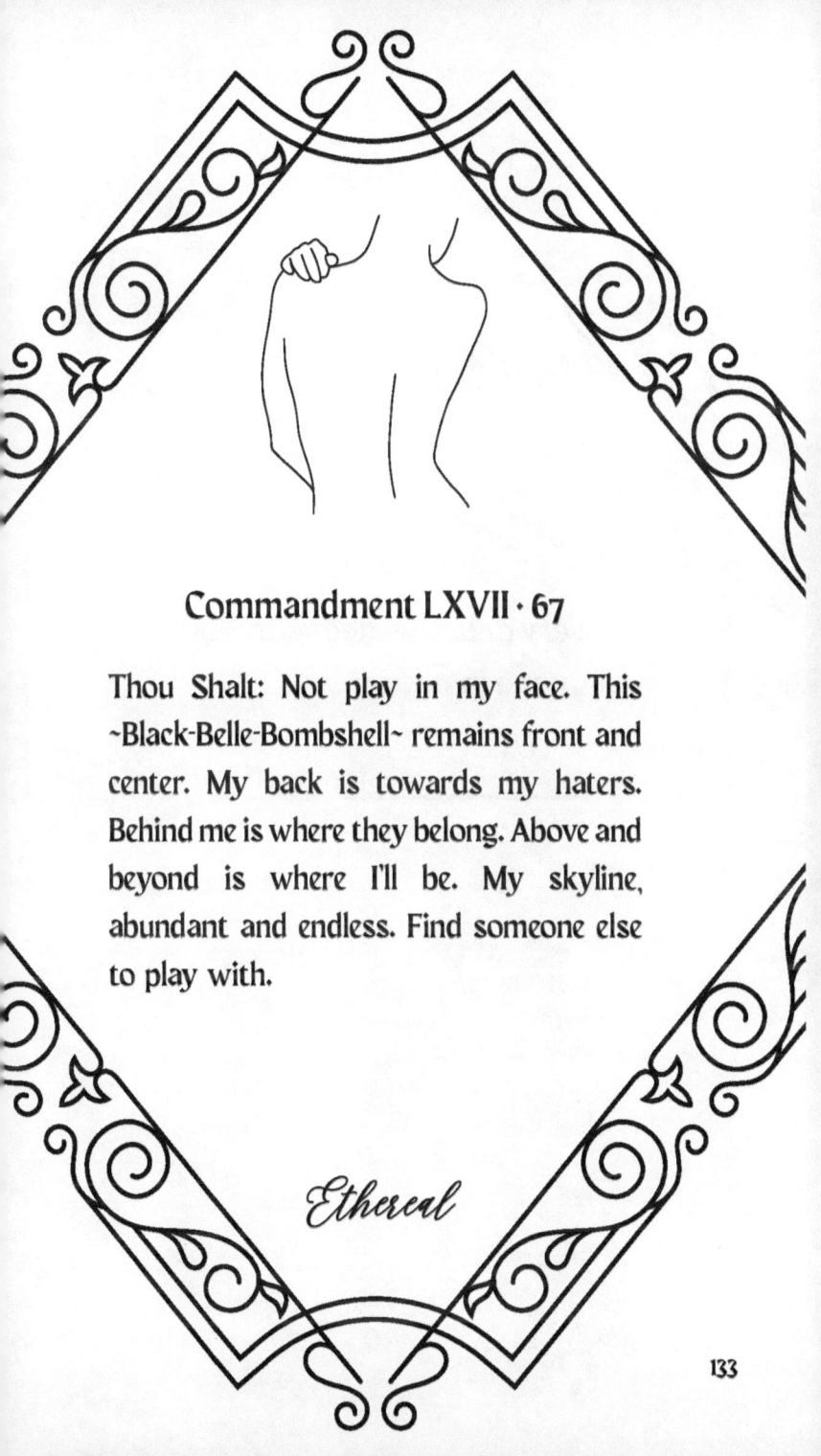

Commandment LXVII · 67

Thou Shalt: Not play in my face. This ~Black-Belle-Bombshell~ remains front and center. My back is towards my haters. Behind me is where they belong. Above and beyond is where I'll be. My skyline, abundant and endless. Find someone else to play with.

Ethereal

Ethereal

Very delicate, heavenly-like,
divine in nature.

Commandment LXVIII · 68

Respect: I am a leader, not a follower. I set trends. I make moves. I drive decisions and make them. I achieve goals. I secure the bag. I am confident. Shall I continue?... Mmm hmm, I shall. I am a boss. I am a winner. I am determined. I am called for greatness. I am fully tapped in. She's woke and on a mission.

Revolutionary

Revolutionary

Bringing about significant, radical change.

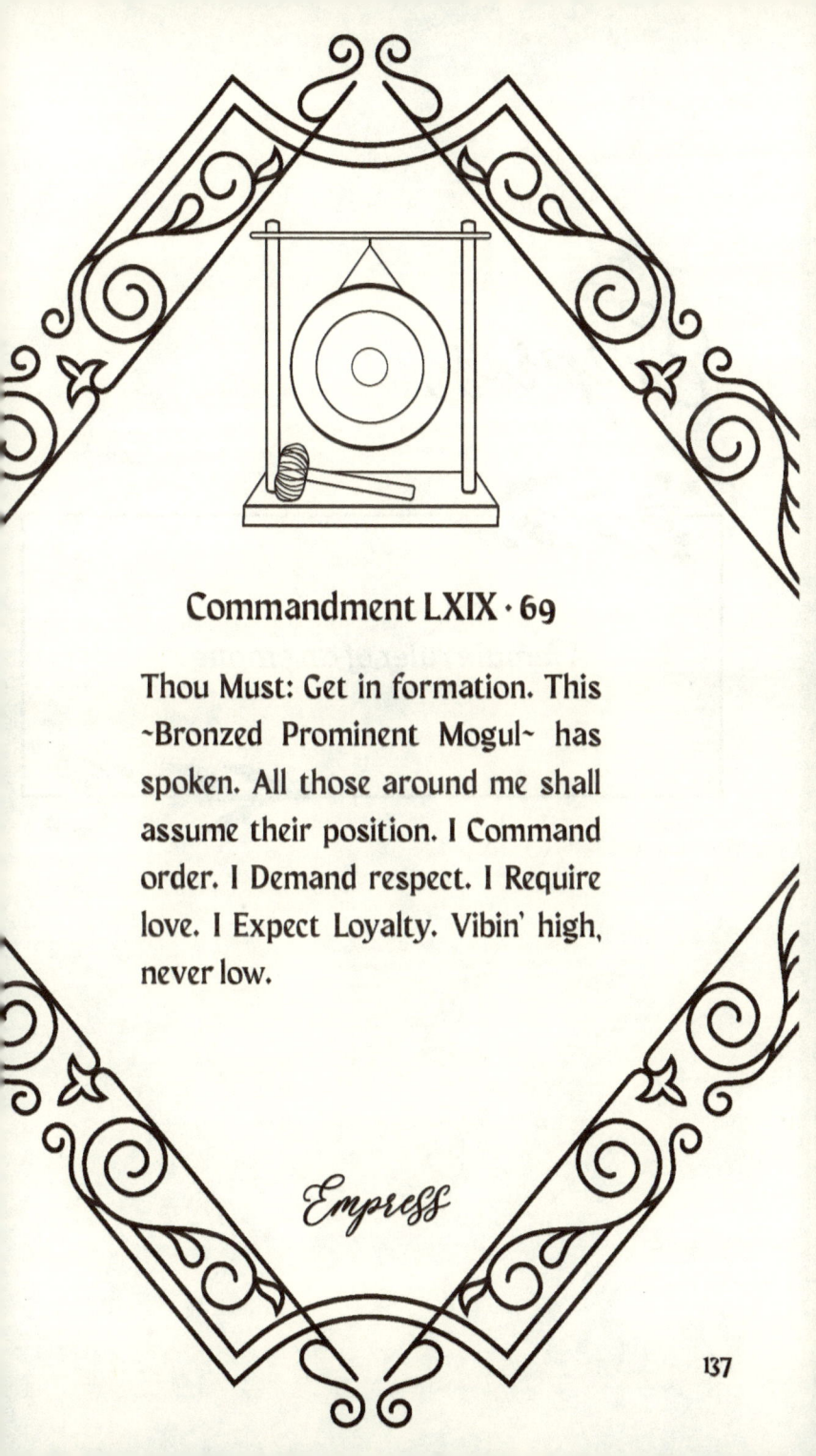

Commandment LXIX · 69

Thou Must: Get in formation. This ~Bronzed Prominent Mogul~ has spoken. All those around me shall assume their position. I Command order. I Demand respect. I Require love. I Expect Loyalty. Vibin' high, never low.

Empress

Empress

A female ruler of an empire.

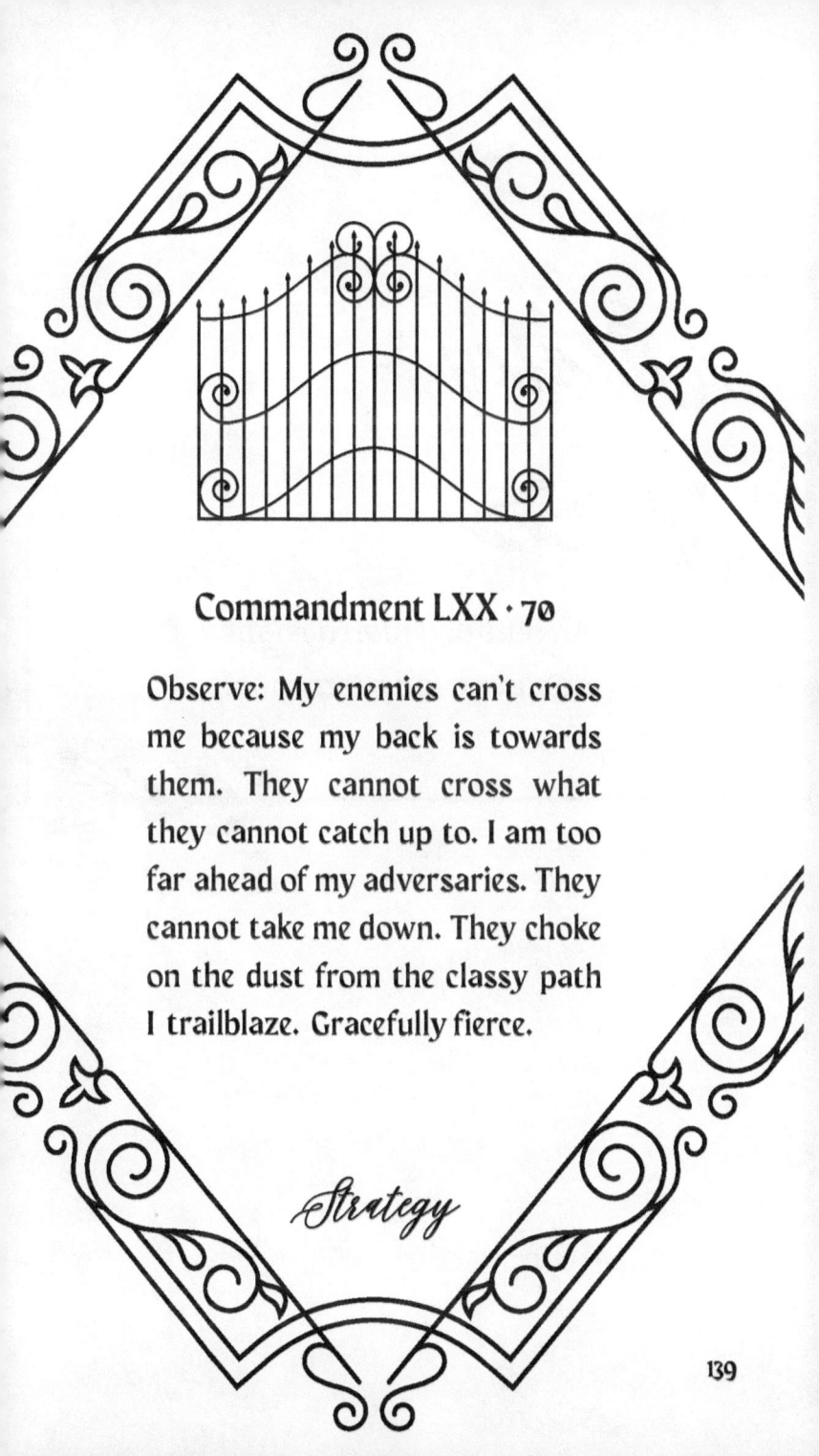

Commandment LXX · 70

Observe: My enemies can't cross me because my back is towards them. They cannot cross what they cannot catch up to. I am too far ahead of my adversaries. They cannot take me down. They choke on the dust from the classy path I trailblaze. Gracefully fierce.

Strategy

Strategy

An outlined plan designed to achieve a long-term goal.

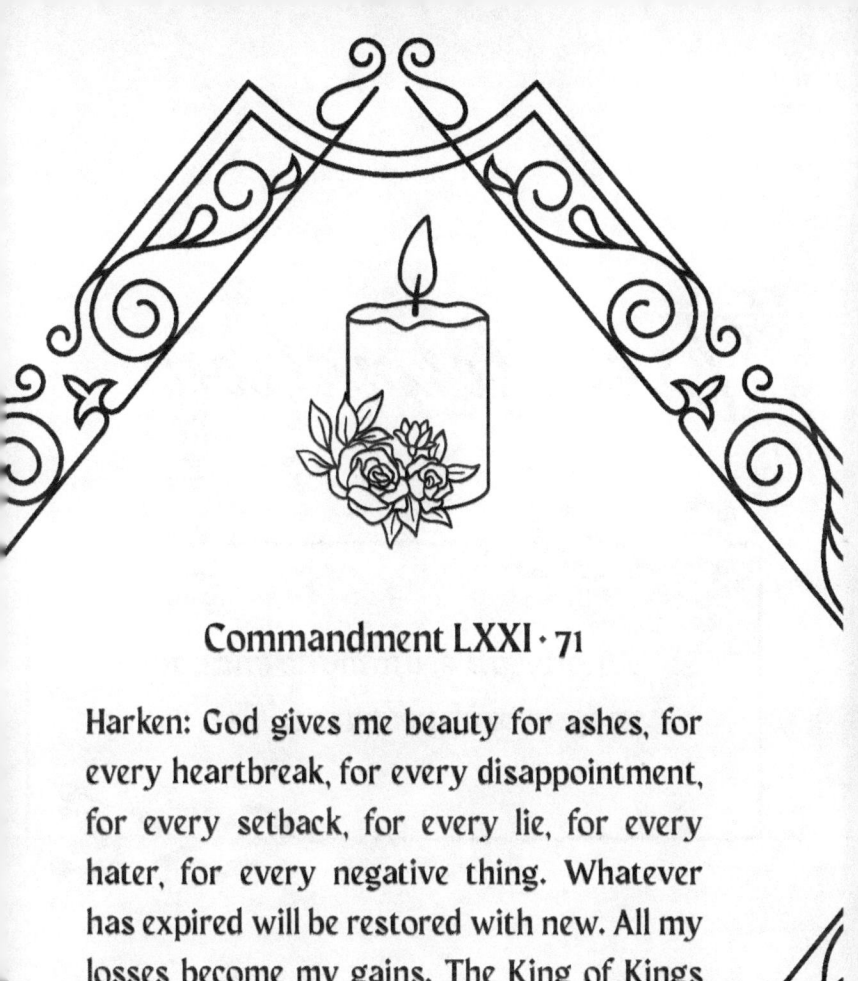

Commandment LXXI · 71

Harken: God gives me beauty for ashes, for every heartbreak, for every disappointment, for every setback, for every lie, for every hater, for every negative thing. Whatever has expired will be restored with new. All my losses become my gains. The King of Kings makes all things right in my life.

Transformation

Transformation

A noticeable, dramatic change in form or appearance.

Commandment LXXII · 72

Thou Shalt: Not catch me slipping. I stay ten steps ahead. I stay rooted in truth. I move with mindful momentum. My ways are wise, my decisions intentional. I climb the ladder with zero slip. I remain firm in my purpose. I am anchored in clarity. I am grounded with grace. I am unmoved by chaos. My inner compass guides me. Led by light, never lost.

Momentum

Momentum

> The driving force that keeps something moving, growing, and going.

Commandment LXXIII · 73

It is Prohibited: Stop trying to figure me out. I am unfigureoutable. This ~Mahogany Madame~ cannot be decoded or defined. I will not do things that are not aligned with my destiny or purpose. I am secure in who I am and what I am called to do. I accept that not everyone will understand. This ~Soul-Enriched Queen~ is carrying on.

Sassy

Sassy

Confident and lively in a
fiery and cheeky way.

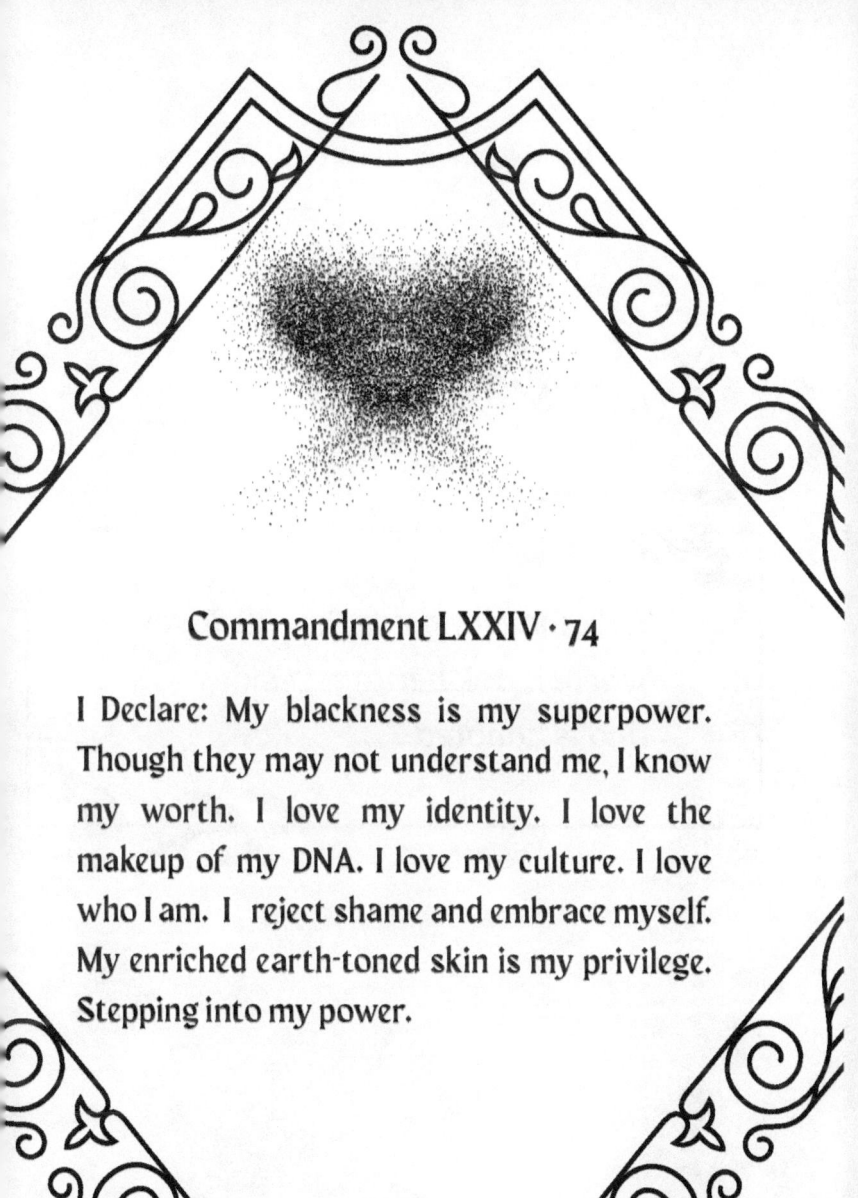

Commandment LXXIV · 74

I Declare: My blackness is my superpower.
Though they may not understand me, I know
my worth. I love my identity. I love the
makeup of my DNA. I love my culture. I love
who I am. I reject shame and embrace myself.
My enriched earth-toned skin is my privilege.
Stepping into my power.

Nubian

Nubian

A region alongside the Nile River
where Black heritage resides
and is honored.

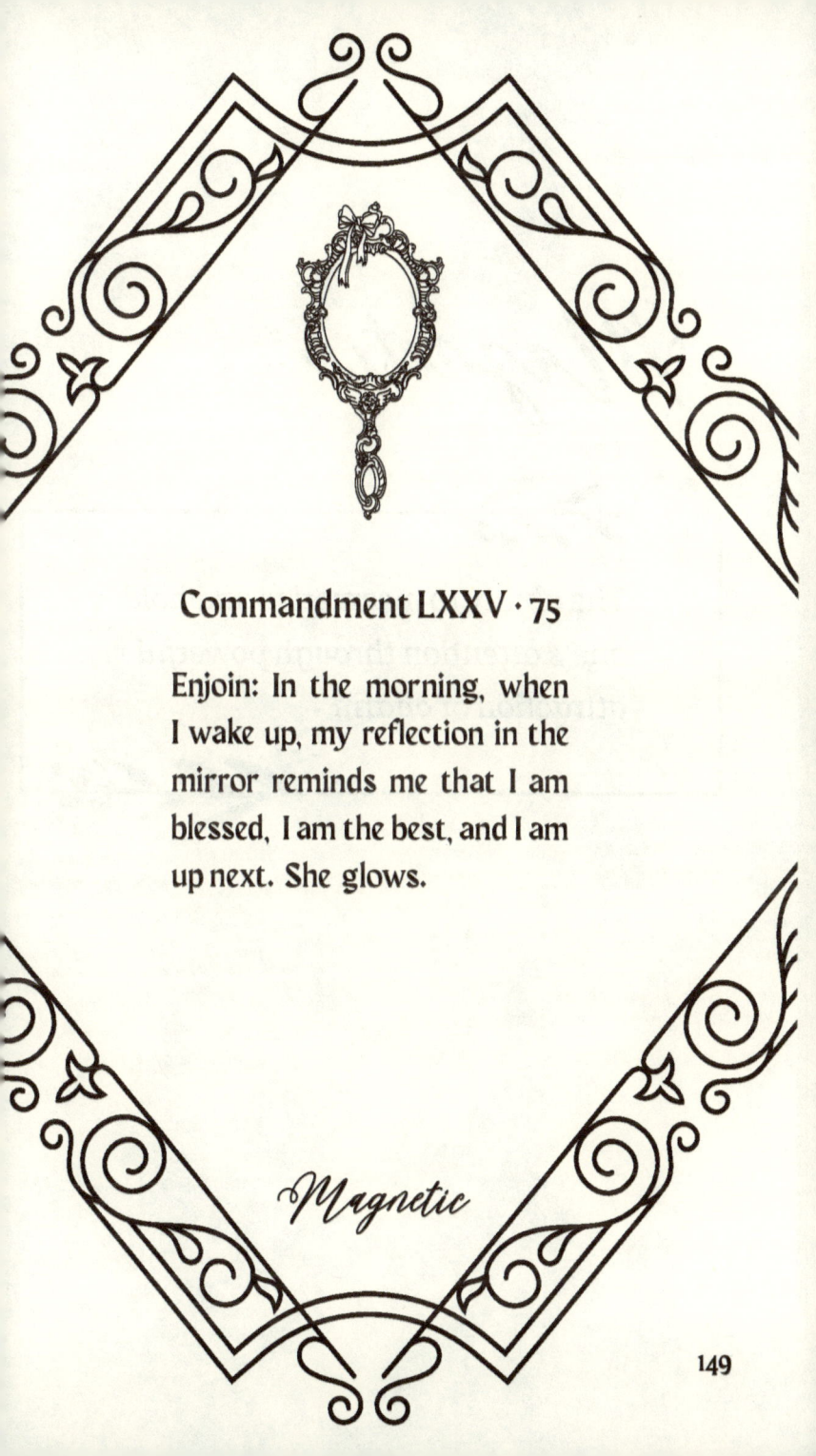

Commandment LXXV · 75

Enjoin: In the morning, when I wake up, my reflection in the mirror reminds me that I am blessed, I am the best, and I am up next. She glows.

Magnetic

Magnetic

The ability to mesmerize and hold one's attention through powerful attraction or charm.

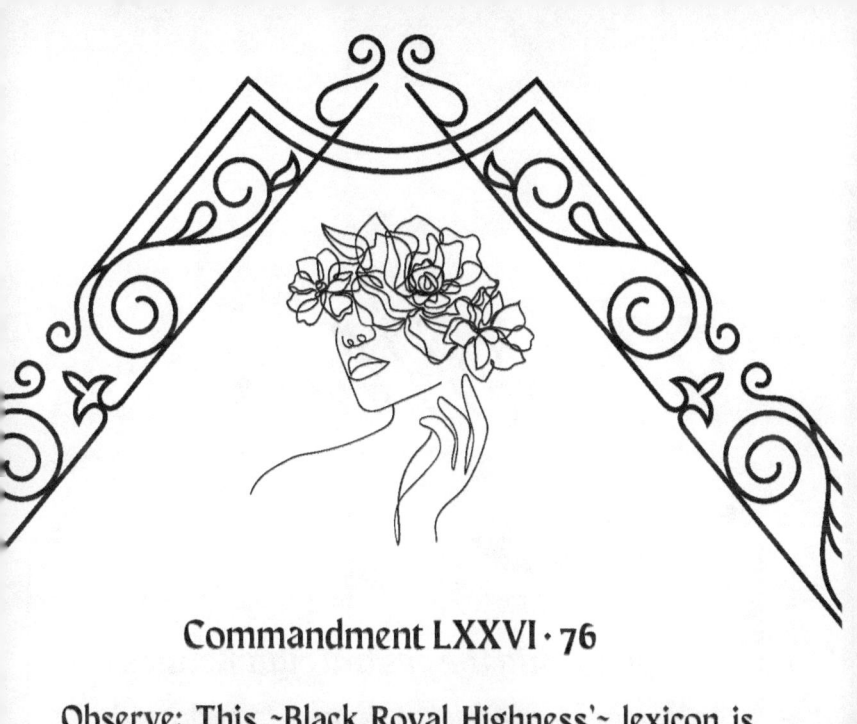

Commandment LXXVI · 76

Observe: This ~Black Royal Highness'~ lexicon is of pleasantries. It speaks life, not death. It articulates freedom, not fear. It asserts power, not pity. It proclaims truth, not illusion. It expresses balance, not breakdown. It conveys focus, not distraction. It opines creation, not destruction. My motherland is in me. ~African Queen~ talk.

Pan-African

Pan-African

Emphasizing the central significance of all people of African descent worldwide.

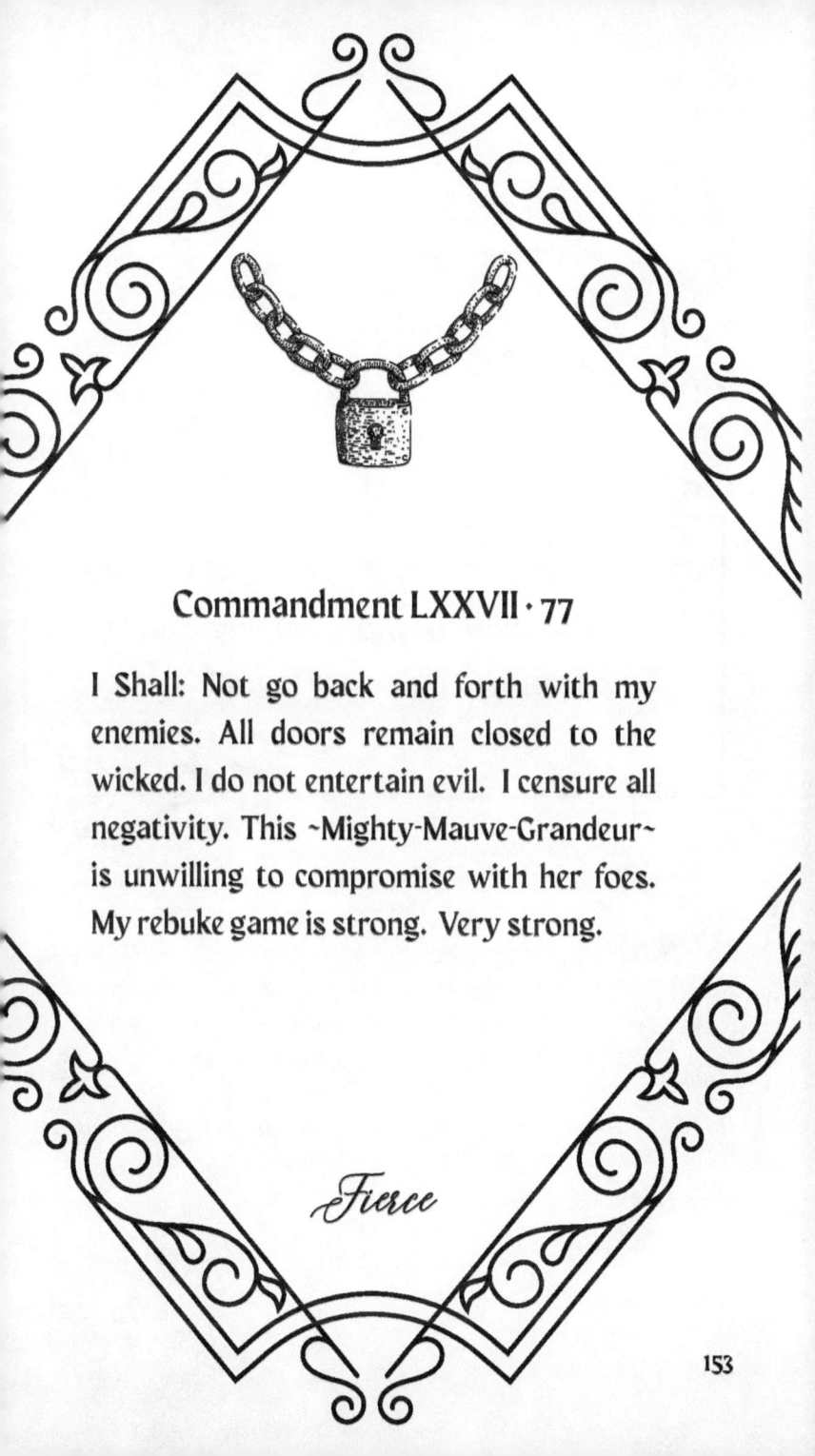

Commandment LXXVII · 77

I Shall: Not go back and forth with my enemies. All doors remain closed to the wicked. I do not entertain evil. I censure all negativity. This ~Mighty-Mauve-Grandeur~ is unwilling to compromise with her foes. My rebuke game is strong. Very strong.

Fierce

Fierce

Filled with power, intensity, and passion in pursuit of a goal.

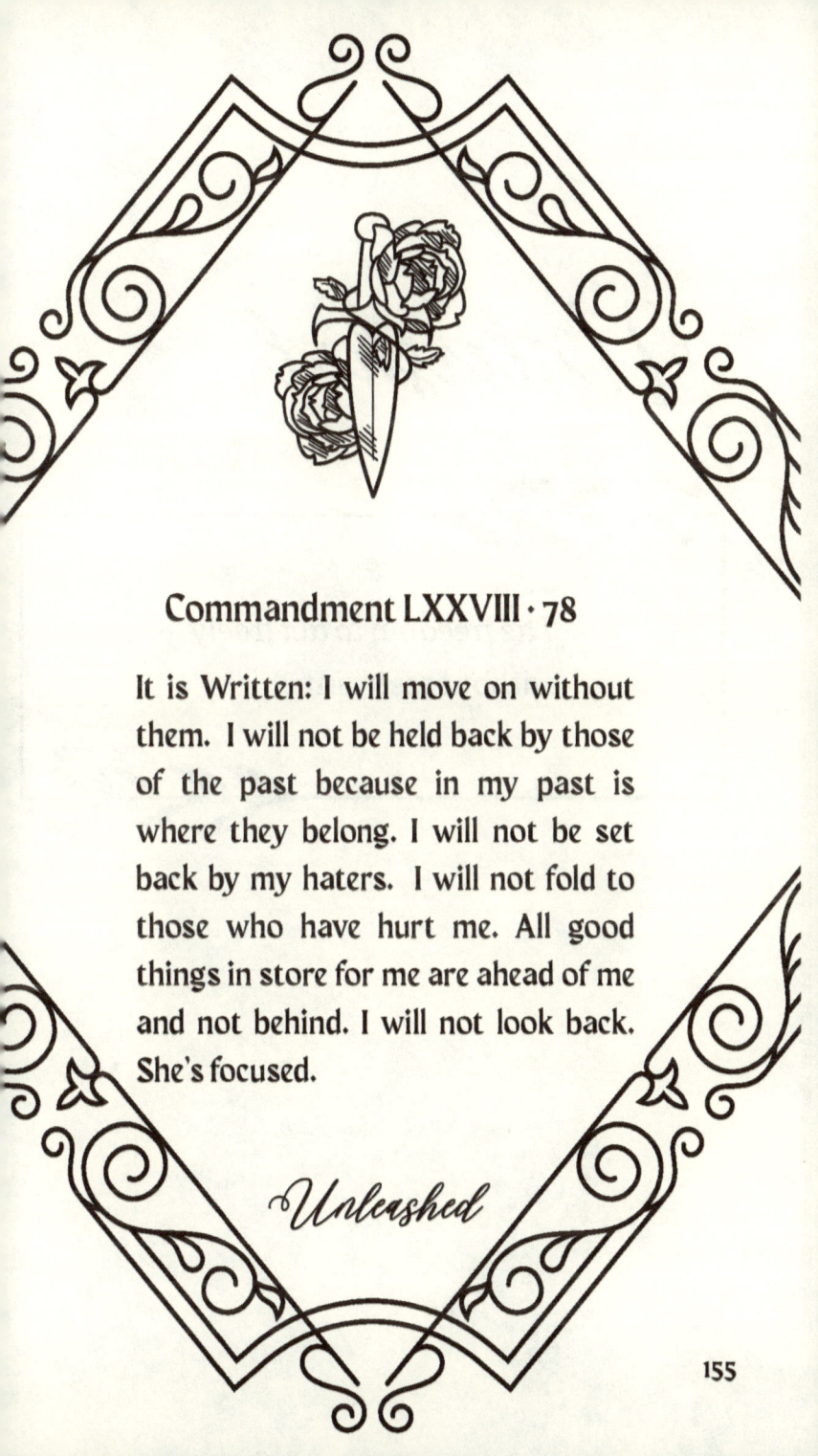

Commandment LXXVIII · 78

It is Written: I will move on without them. I will not be held back by those of the past because in my past is where they belong. I will not be set back by my haters. I will not fold to those who have hurt me. All good things in store for me are ahead of me and not behind. I will not look back. She's focused.

Unleashed

Unleashed

The freedom to act freely
without restraint.

Commandment LXXIX · 79

Observe: This ~Supreme Soul-Sista~ is consistent, persistent, and determined. I secure the bag. I make the right decisions. I make the right moves. I close all deals. I build my empire effortlessly. I am a bold blueprint builder. Watch me construct. Watch me grow. She's activated.

Monarch

Monarch

A person of royal status who rules or has powers over others.

Commandment LXXX · 80

Thou Shalt: Respect my authority. This ~Black Benevolent Queen~ requires respect. I do not tolerate foolishness. I do not entertain debauchery. I do not indulge in immorality. My path is straight and not crooked. I stand on big principles. I stand on big values. I gather my critics. I block my opposition. I discard my dissenters. Put some respect on it.

Dominant

Dominant

Exercising power and
influence over others.

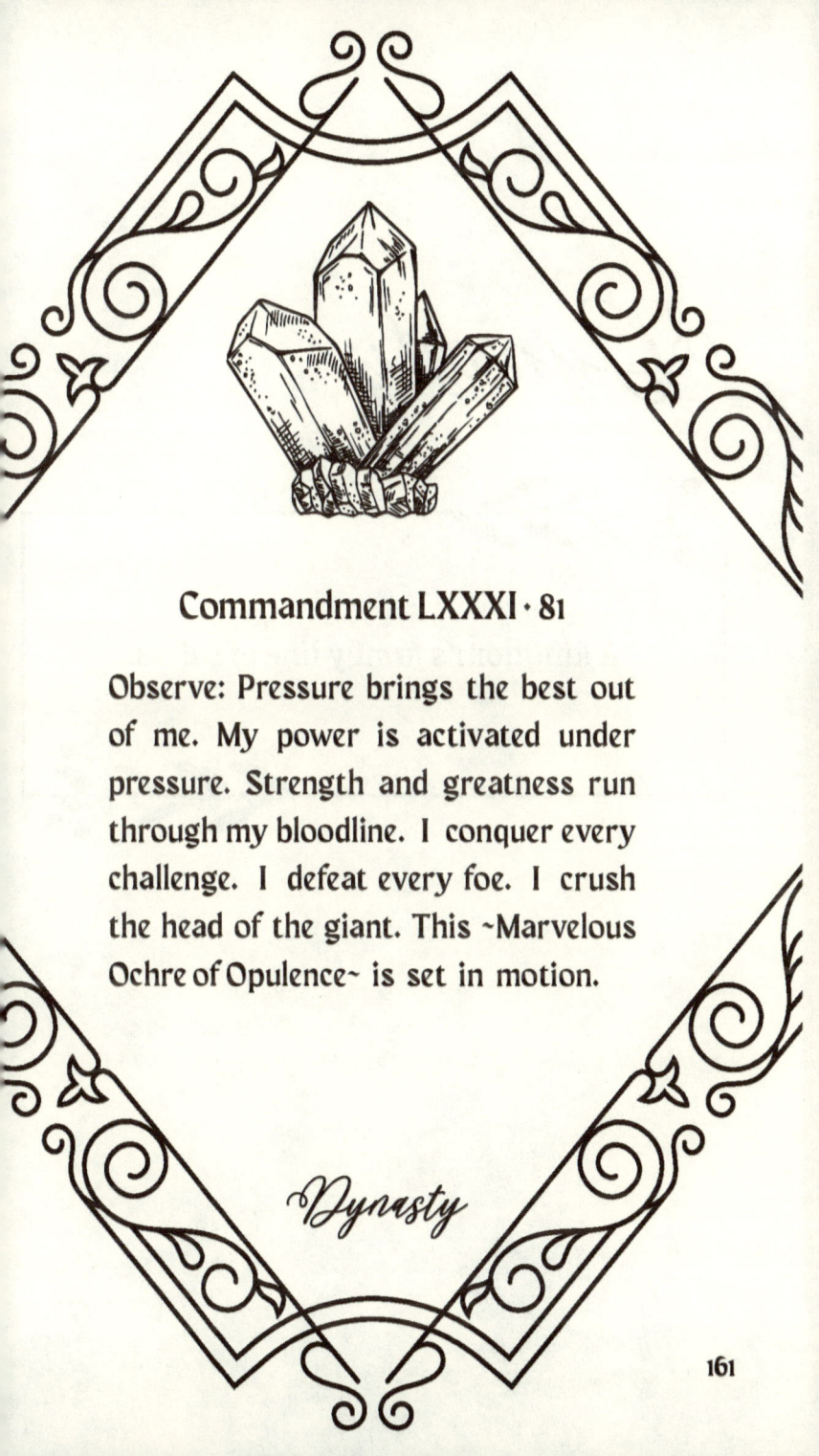

Commandment LXXXI · 81

Observe: Pressure brings the best out of me. My power is activated under pressure. Strength and greatness run through my bloodline. I conquer every challenge. I defeat every foe. I crush the head of the giant. This ~Marvelous Ochre of Opulence~ is set in motion.

Dynasty

Dynasty

A kingdom's family line of rulers.

Commandment LXXXII · 82

I Acknowledge: Unlike them, I take results over likes. Likes, hearts, emojis and thumbs up do not validate this ~Black Diamond Empress~, only my realizations. Legacy over likes. Get into it.

Purpose

Purpose

The intention or driving force behind why something is desired or accomplished.

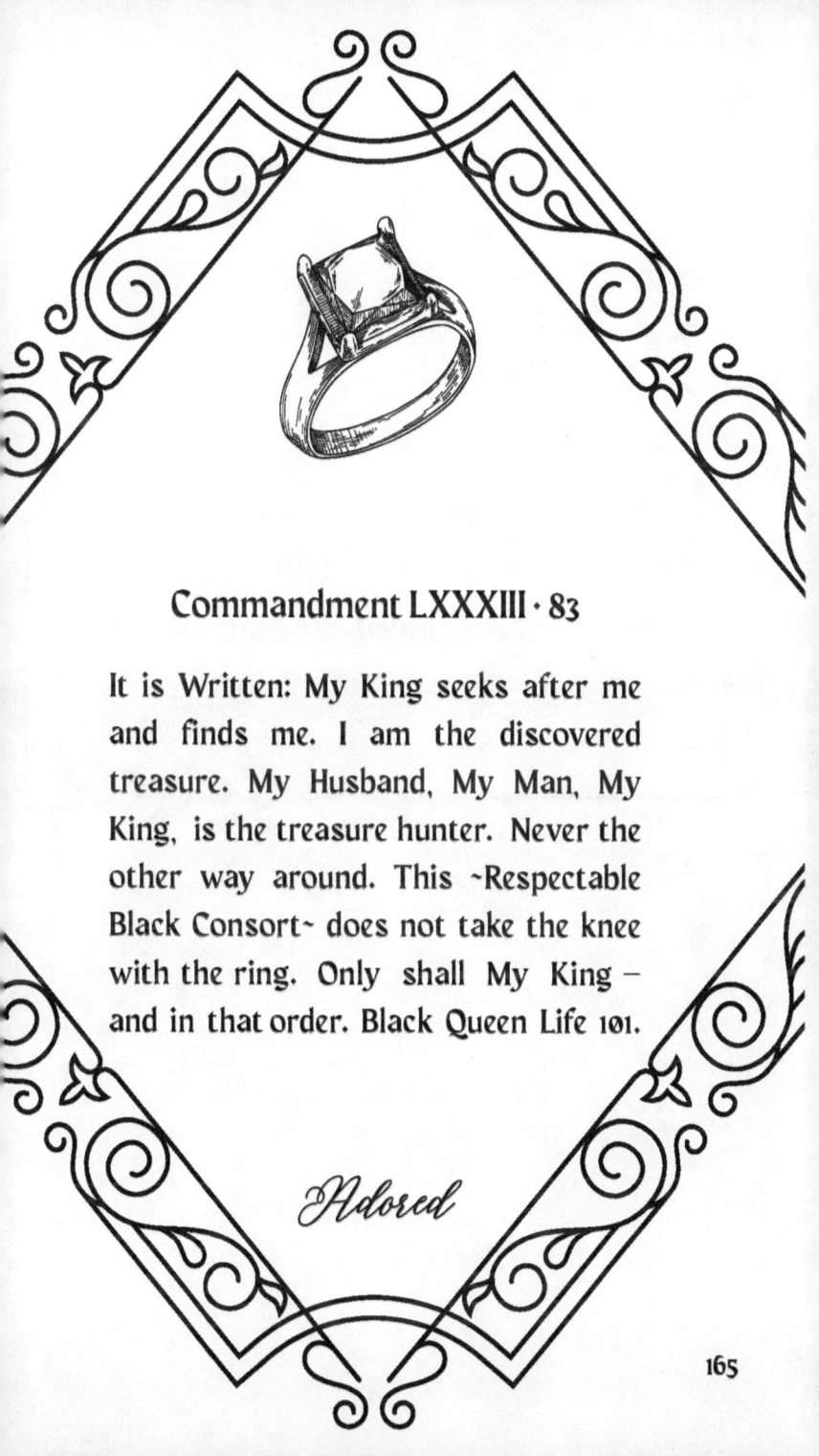

Commandment LXXXIII · 83

It is Written: My King seeks after me and finds me. I am the discovered treasure. My Husband, My Man, My King, is the treasure hunter. Never the other way around. This ~Respectable Black Consort~ does not take the knee with the ring. Only shall My King — and in that order. Black Queen Life 101.

Adored

Adored

*Deeply loved, revered,
esteemed, and worthy.*

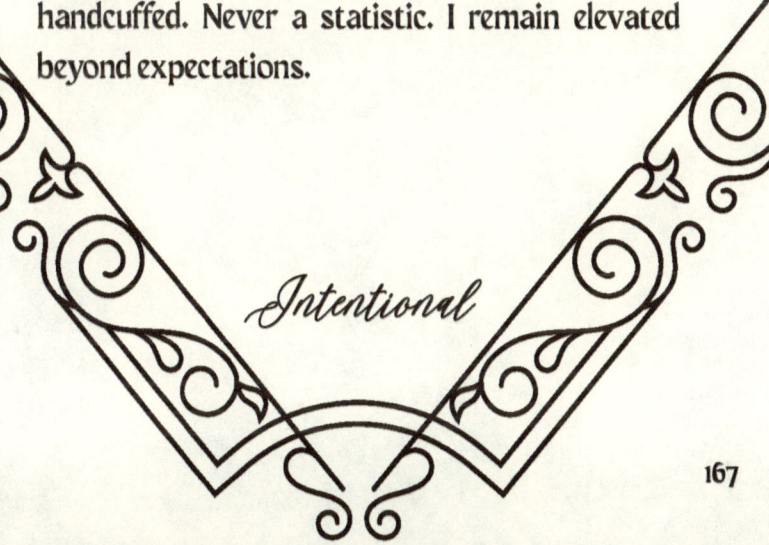

Commandment LXXXIV · 84

Take Heed: I will not be 'Arrested Development.' This ~Umber-Toned Regent~ lives in a forever state of learning, growing, and evolving. Never repressed. Never oppressed. Never dense. Never strained. Never stifled. Never thwarted. Never handcuffed. Never a statistic. I remain elevated beyond expectations.

Intentional

Intentional

*Being purposeful in nature
with a clear aim or plan.*

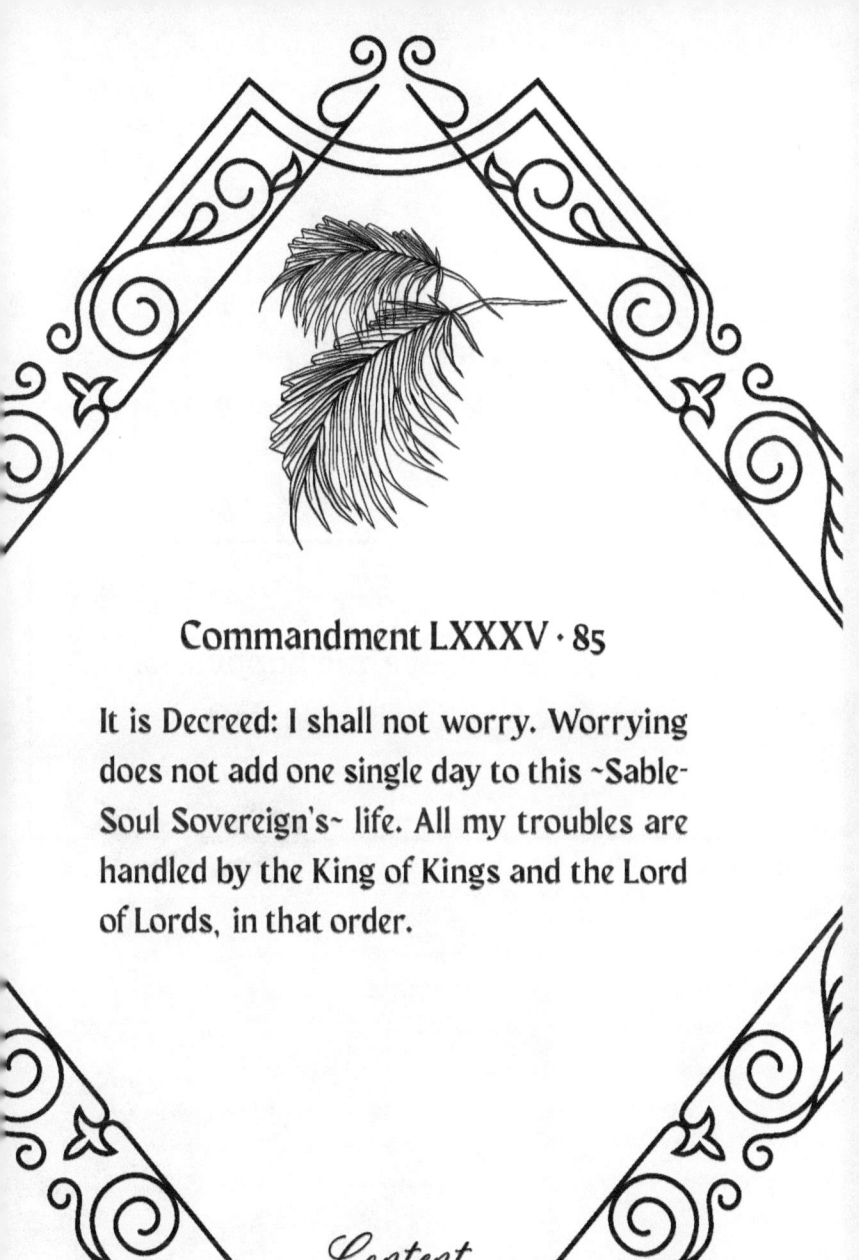

Commandment LXXXV · 85

It is Decreed: I shall not worry. Worrying does not add one single day to this ~Sable-Soul Sovereign's~ life. All my troubles are handled by the King of Kings and the Lord of Lords, in that order.

Content

Content

The state of peace and happiness, having an optimistic mindset.

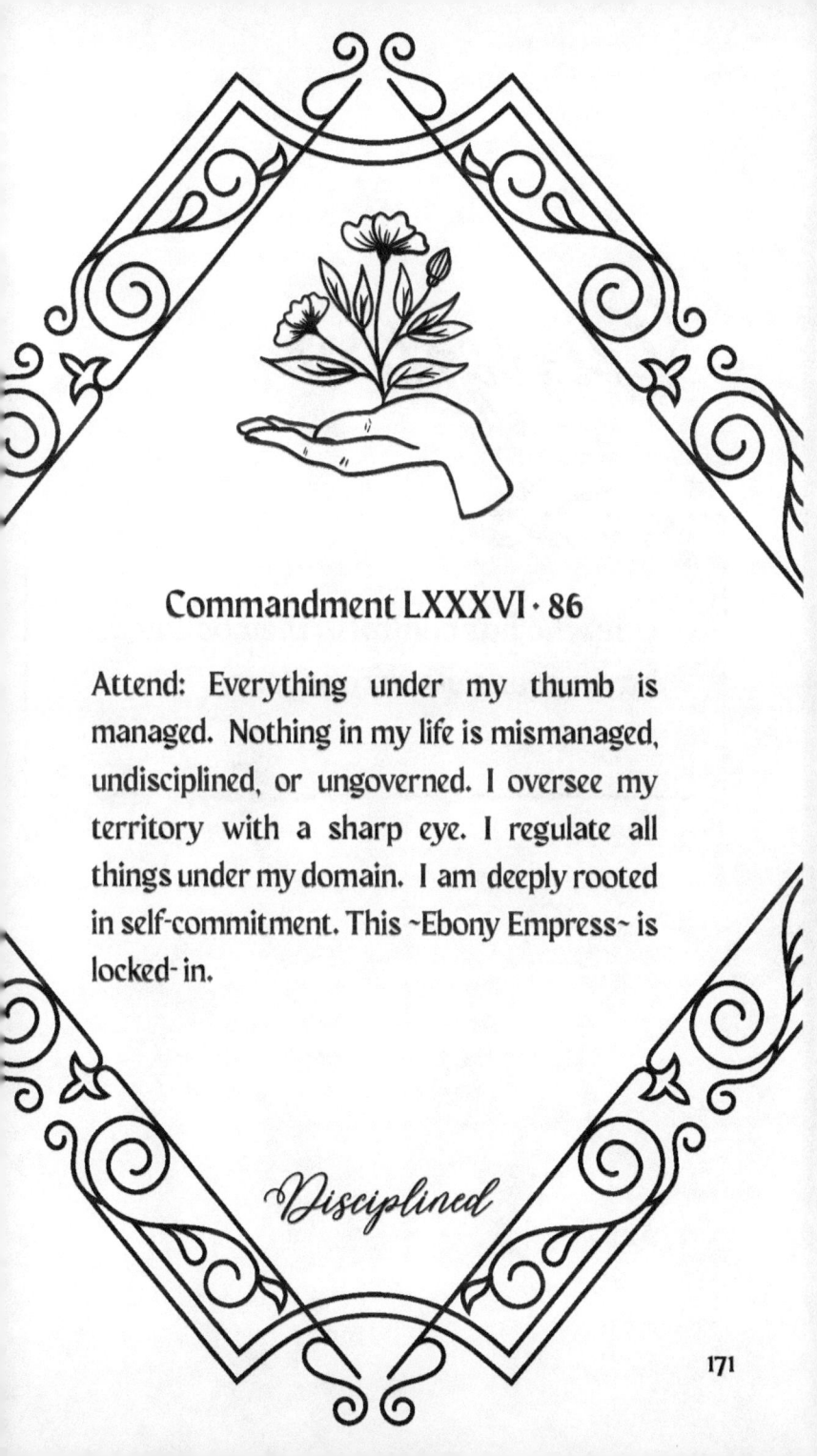

Commandment LXXXVI · 86

Attend: Everything under my thumb is managed. Nothing in my life is mismanaged, undisciplined, or ungoverned. I oversee my territory with a sharp eye. I regulate all things under my domain. I am deeply rooted in self-commitment. This ~Ebony Empress~ is locked-in.

Disciplined

Disciplined

One who has control in their behavior, having consistency and focus.

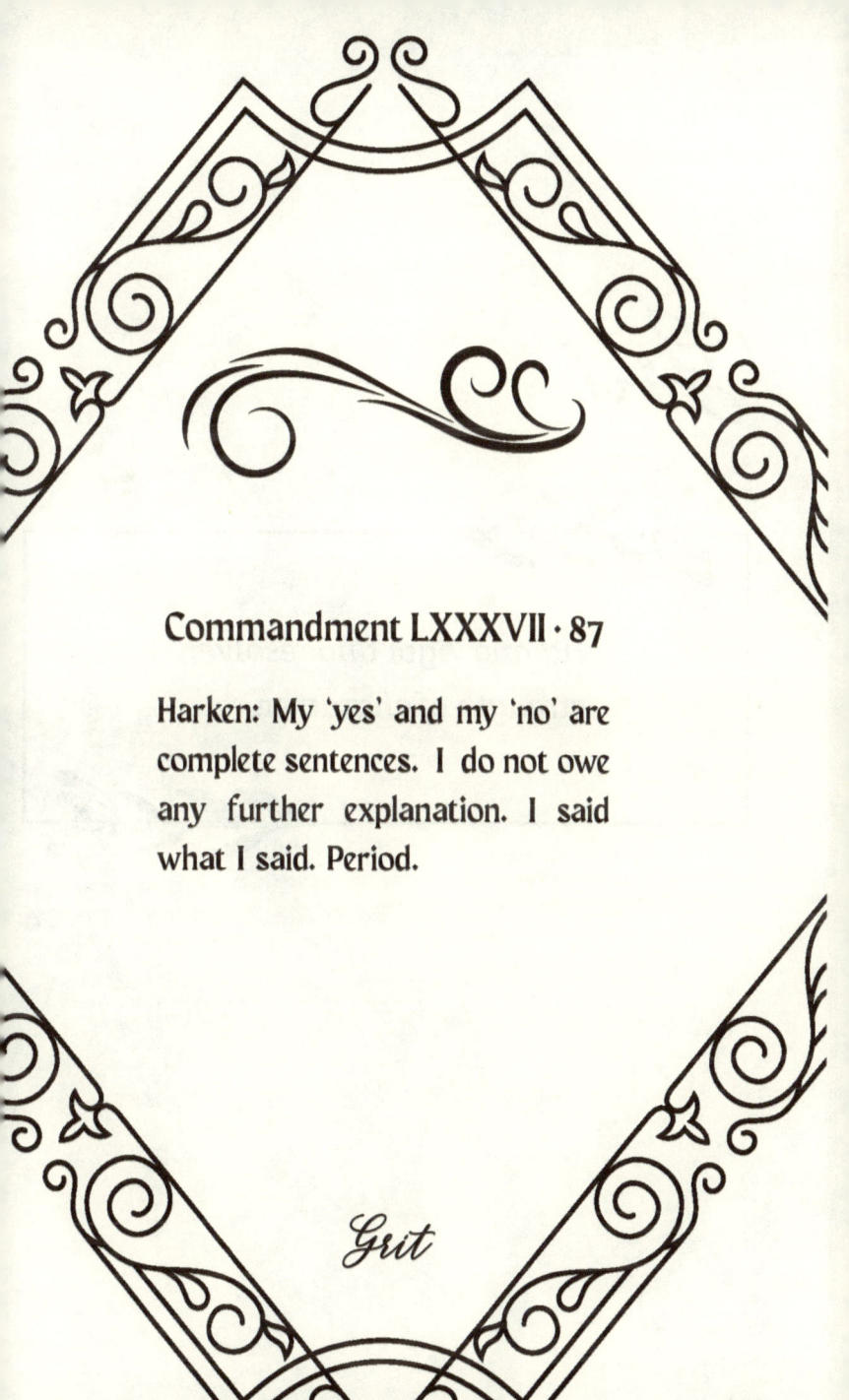

Commandment LXXXVII · 87

Harken: My 'yes' and my 'no' are complete sentences. I do not owe any further explanation. I said what I said. Period.

Grit

Grit

Having vigor and resolve;
strength of character.

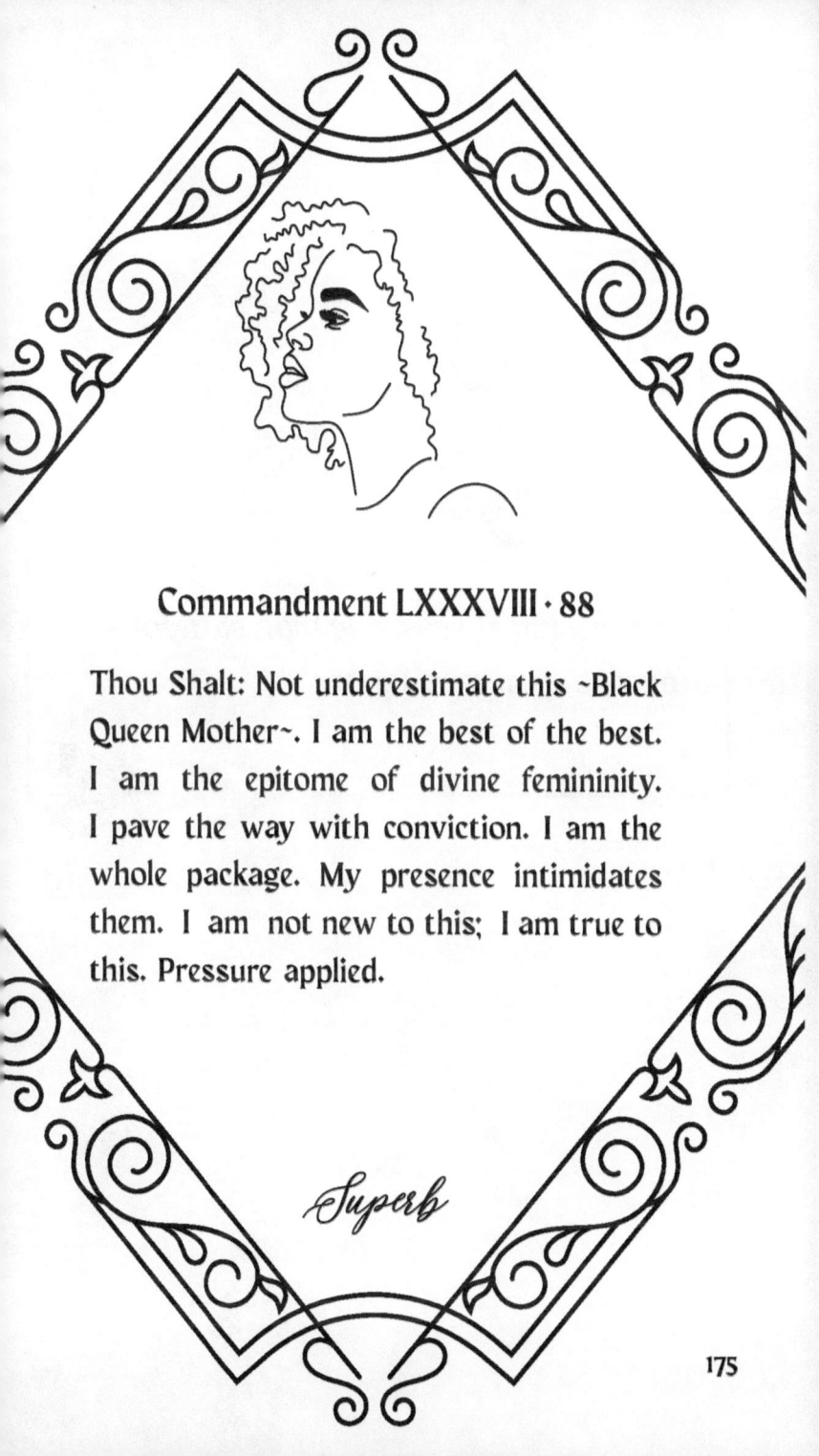

Commandment LXXXVIII · 88

Thou Shalt: Not underestimate this ~Black Queen Mother~. I am the best of the best. I am the epitome of divine femininity. I pave the way with conviction. I am the whole package. My presence intimidates them. I am not new to this; I am true to this. Pressure applied.

Superb

Superb

Possessing obsessively high standards, operating in excellence.

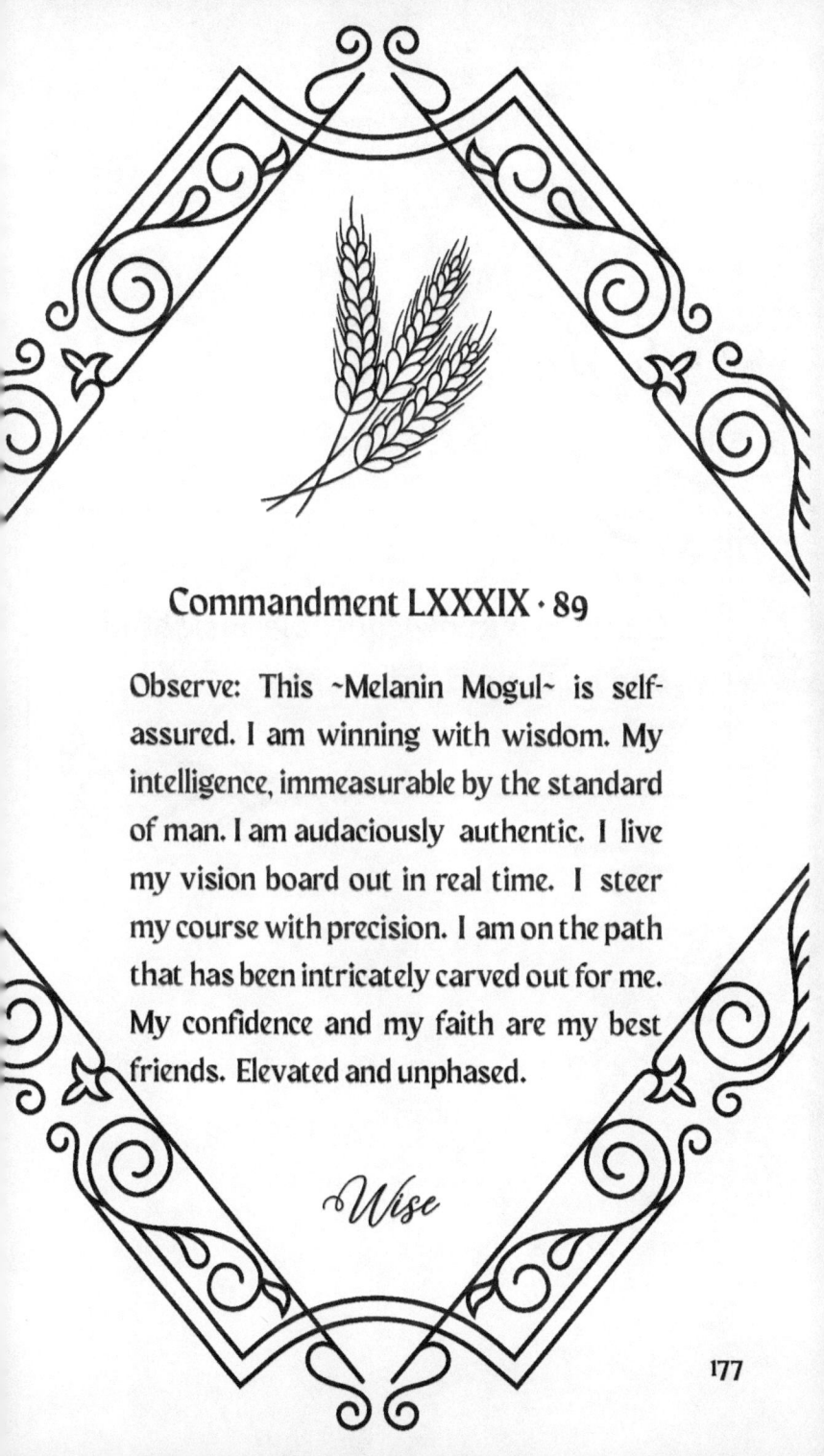

Commandment LXXXIX · 89

Observe: This ~Melanin Mogul~ is self-assured. I am winning with wisdom. My intelligence, immeasurable by the standard of man. I am audaciously authentic. I live my vision board out in real time. I steer my course with precision. I am on the path that has been intricately carved out for me. My confidence and my faith are my best friends. Elevated and unphased.

Wise

Wise

One who is knowledgeable, insightful, and has sound judgment.

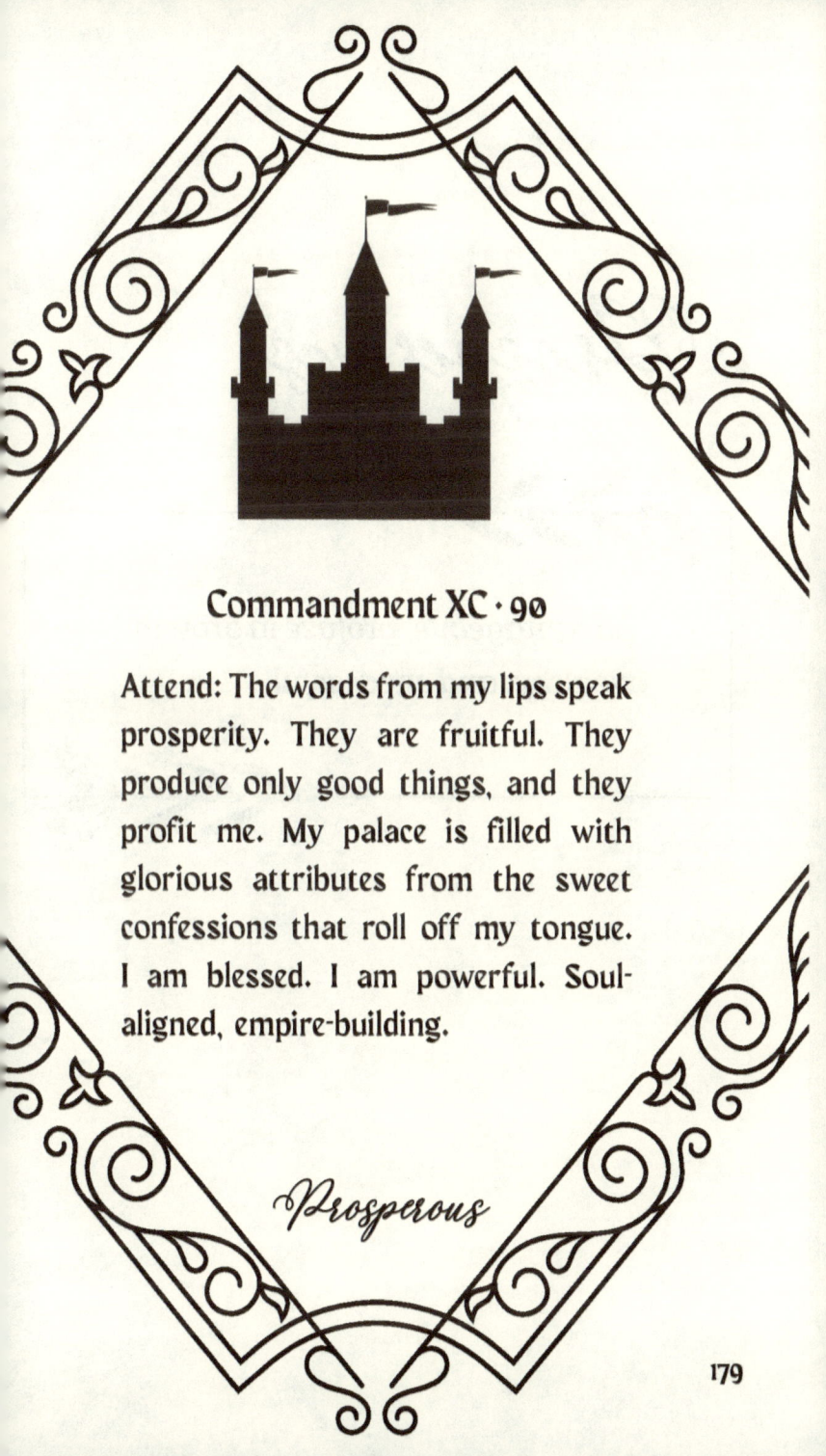

Commandment XC · 90

Attend: The words from my lips speak prosperity. They are fruitful. They produce only good things, and they profit me. My palace is filled with glorious attributes from the sweet confessions that roll off my tongue. I am blessed. I am powerful. Soul-aligned, empire-building.

Prosperous

Prosperous

Advantageous, profuse in growth,
wealthy, and successful.

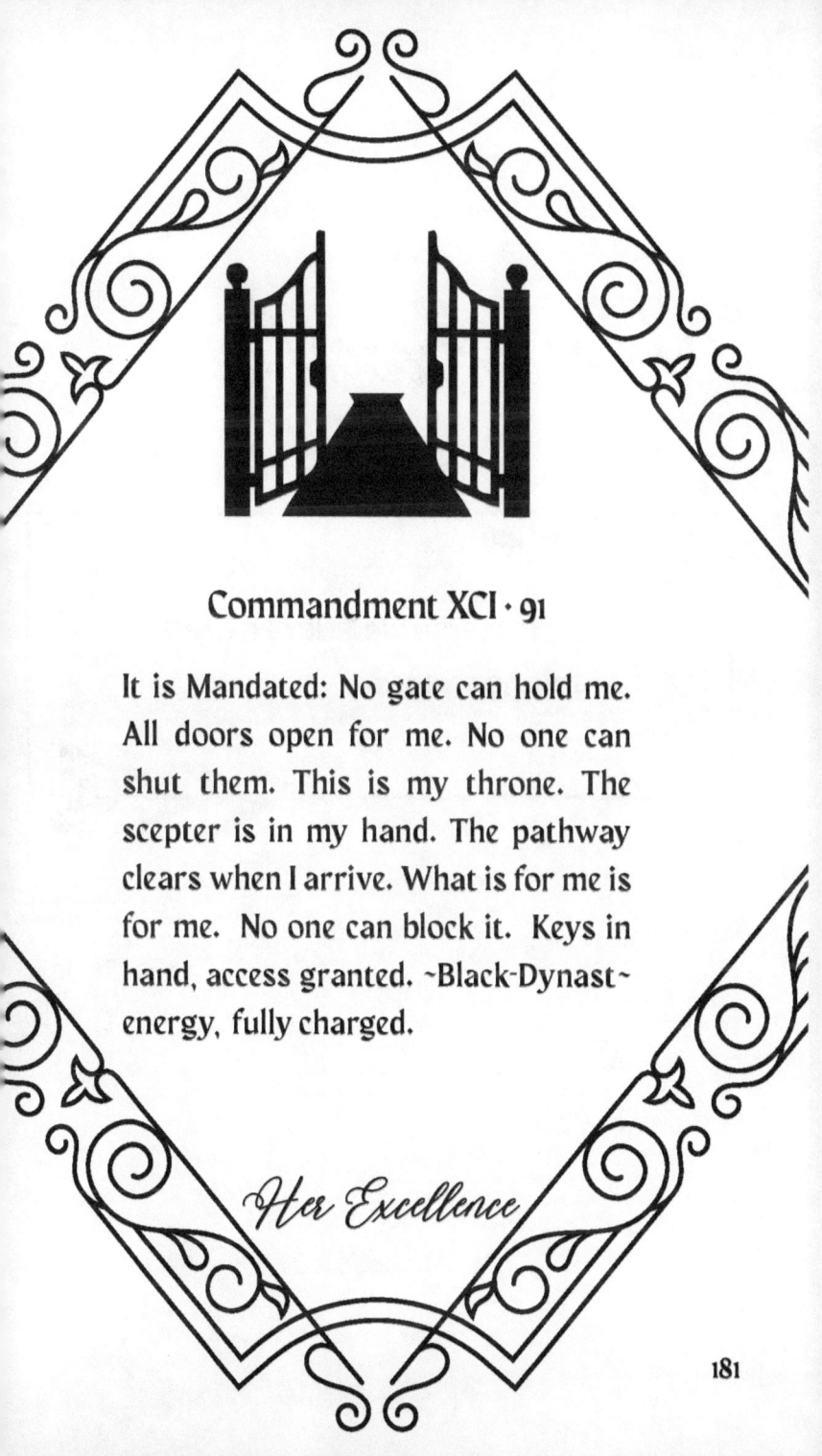

Commandment XCI · 91

It is Mandated: No gate can hold me. All doors open for me. No one can shut them. This is my throne. The scepter is in my hand. The pathway clears when I arrive. What is for me is for me. No one can block it. Keys in hand, access granted. ~Black-Dynast~ energy, fully charged.

Her Excellence

Her Excellence

The respectable title of a high-ranking woman.

Commandment XCII · 92

Take Heed: My destiny is not delayed. Everything is right on time for me. I make intelligent decisions. I make power moves. My life is aligned. The sky is the limit for this ~Golden-Hued Regent~. Watch me fly.

Aligned

Aligned

Synced and working
together effectively.

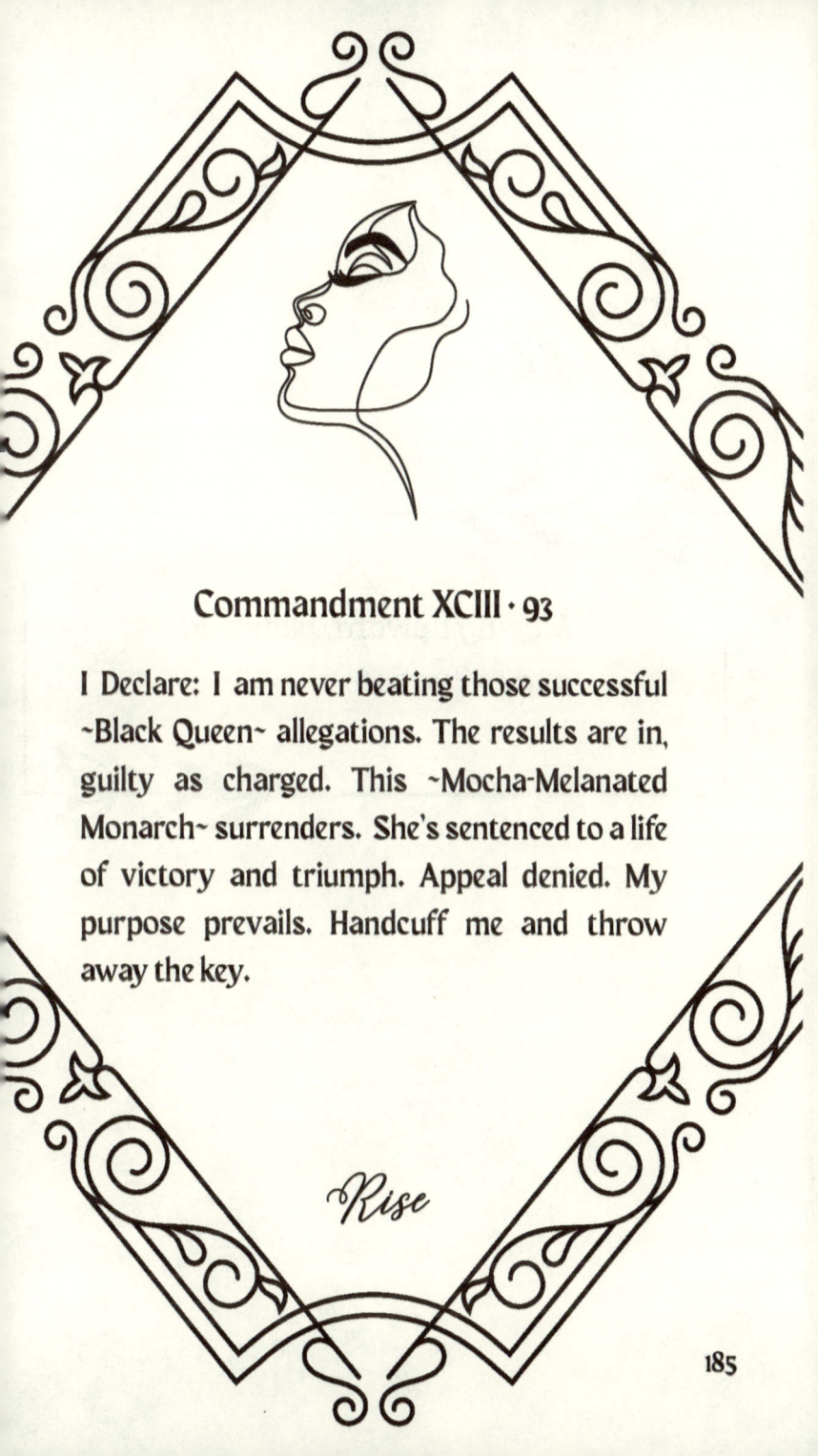

Commandment XCIII · 93

I Declare: I am never beating those successful ~Black Queen~ allegations. The results are in, guilty as charged. This ~Mocha-Melanated Monarch~ surrenders. She's sentenced to a life of victory and triumph. Appeal denied. My purpose prevails. Handcuff me and throw away the key.

Rise

Rise

Moving upward, bettering one's situation.

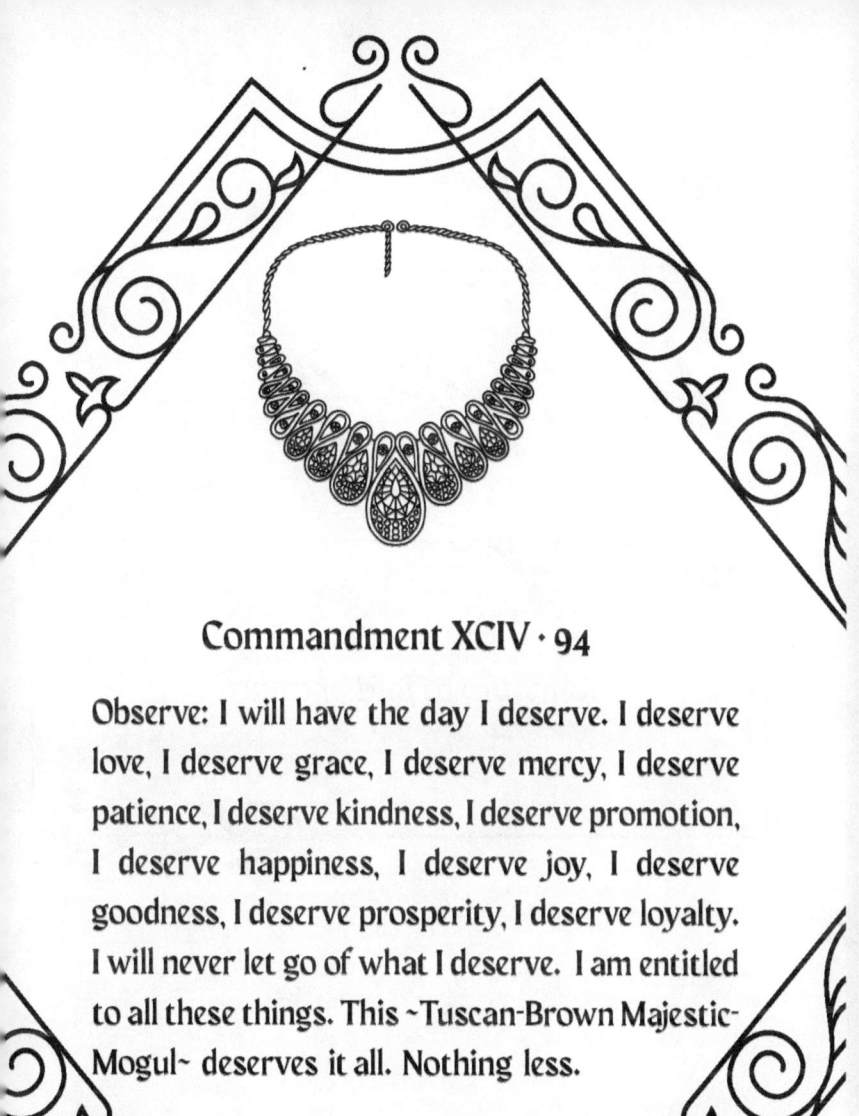

Commandment XCIV · 94

Observe: I will have the day I deserve. I deserve love, I deserve grace, I deserve mercy, I deserve patience, I deserve kindness, I deserve promotion, I deserve happiness, I deserve joy, I deserve goodness, I deserve prosperity, I deserve loyalty. I will never let go of what I deserve. I am entitled to all these things. This ~Tuscan-Brown Majestic-Mogul~ deserves it all. Nothing less.

Unyielding

Unyielding

Refusing to fold or give in.

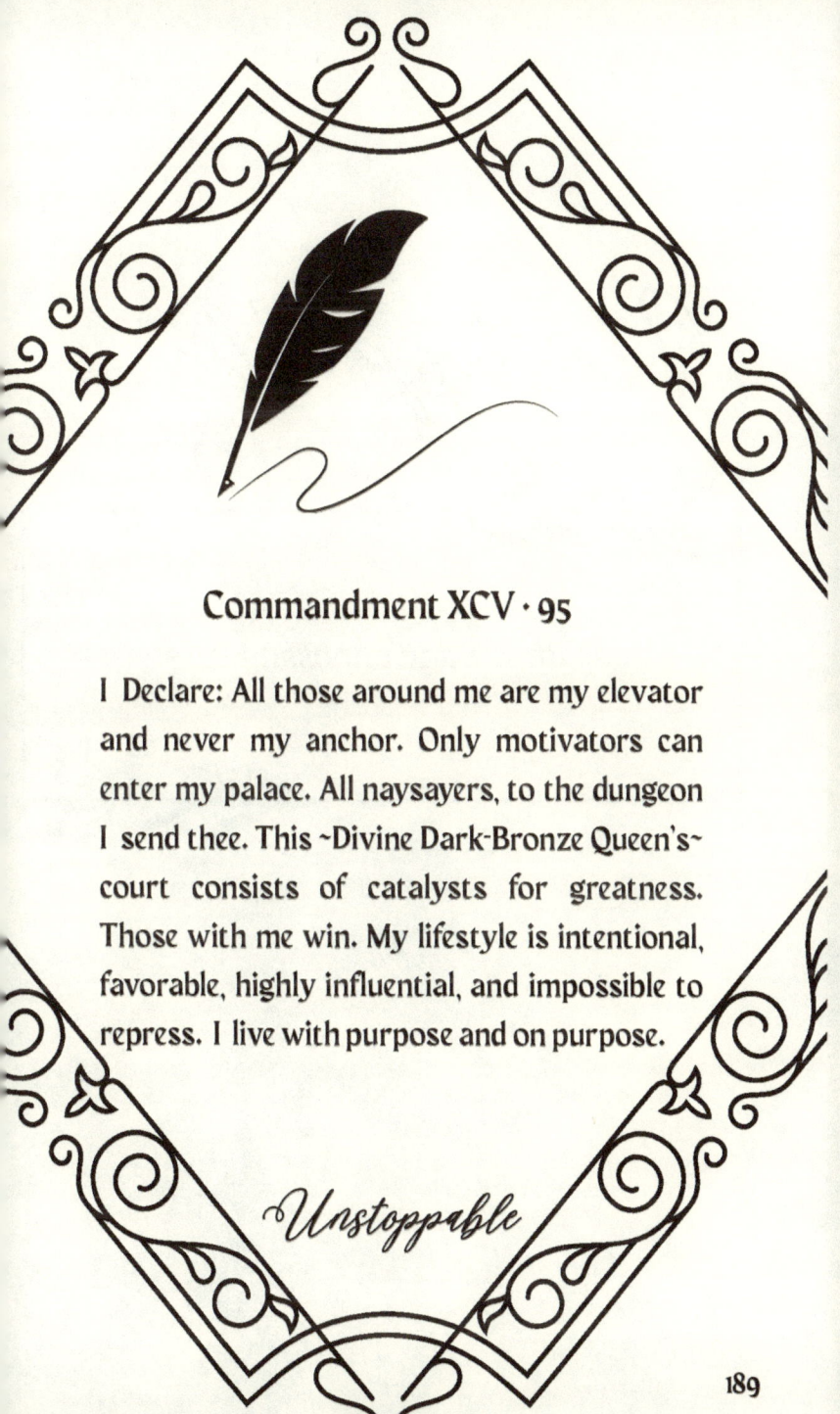

Commandment XCV · 95

I Declare: All those around me are my elevator and never my anchor. Only motivators can enter my palace. All naysayers, to the dungeon I send thee. This ~Divine Dark-Bronze Queen's~ court consists of catalysts for greatness. Those with me win. My lifestyle is intentional, favorable, highly influential, and impossible to repress. I live with purpose and on purpose.

Unstoppable

Unstoppable

Undefeatable and impossible to stop.

Commandment XCVI · 96

It is Prohibited: Critics can't hold me back. I'm still here. This Queen is in it for the long haul. I am a Conqueror. I am Victorious. They can't block this ~Great Black Dame~ from succeeding. Impossible.

Resilient

Resilient

Having a strong comeback from setbacks and tough times.

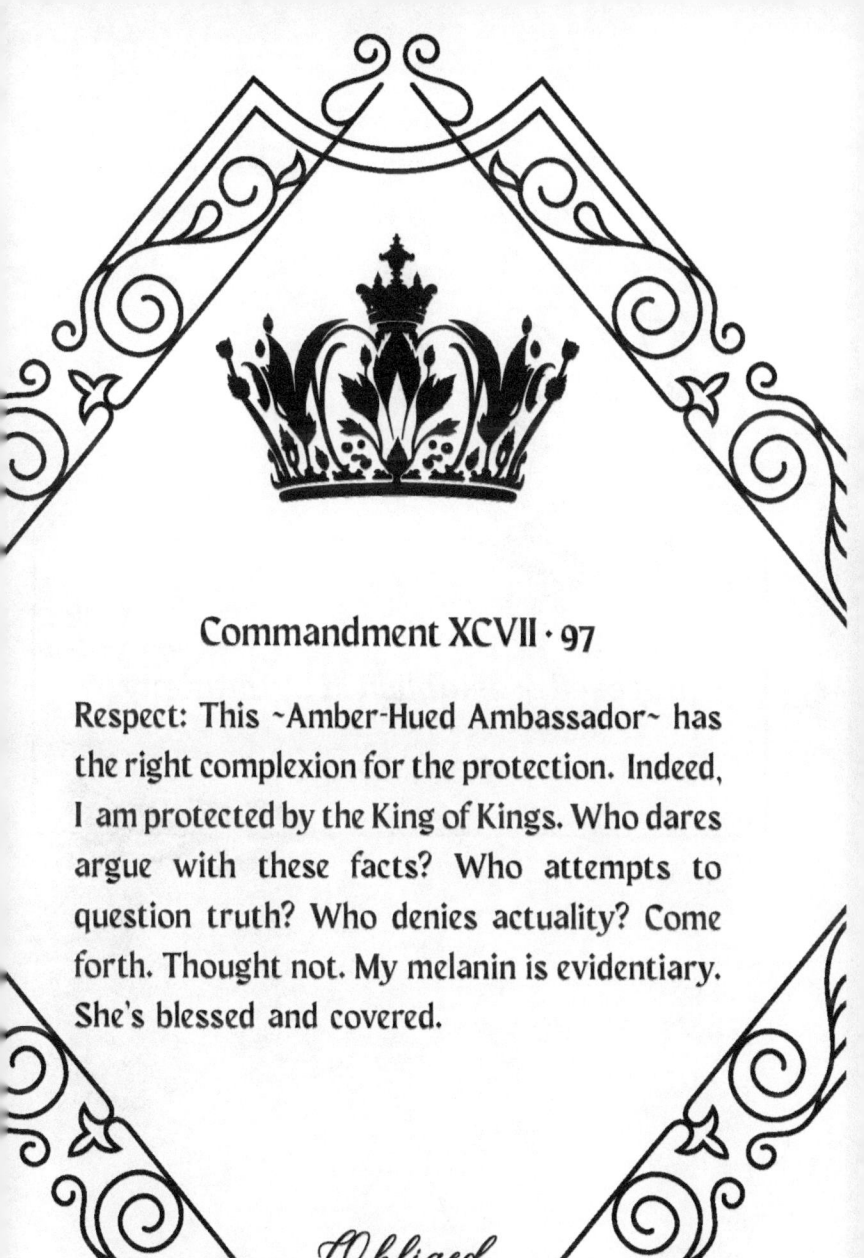

Commandment XCVII · 97

Respect: This ~Amber-Hued Ambassador~ has the right complexion for the protection. Indeed, I am protected by the King of Kings. Who dares argue with these facts? Who attempts to question truth? Who denies actuality? Come forth. Thought not. My melanin is evidentiary. She's blessed and covered.

Obliged

Obliged

Imposed or established by authority.

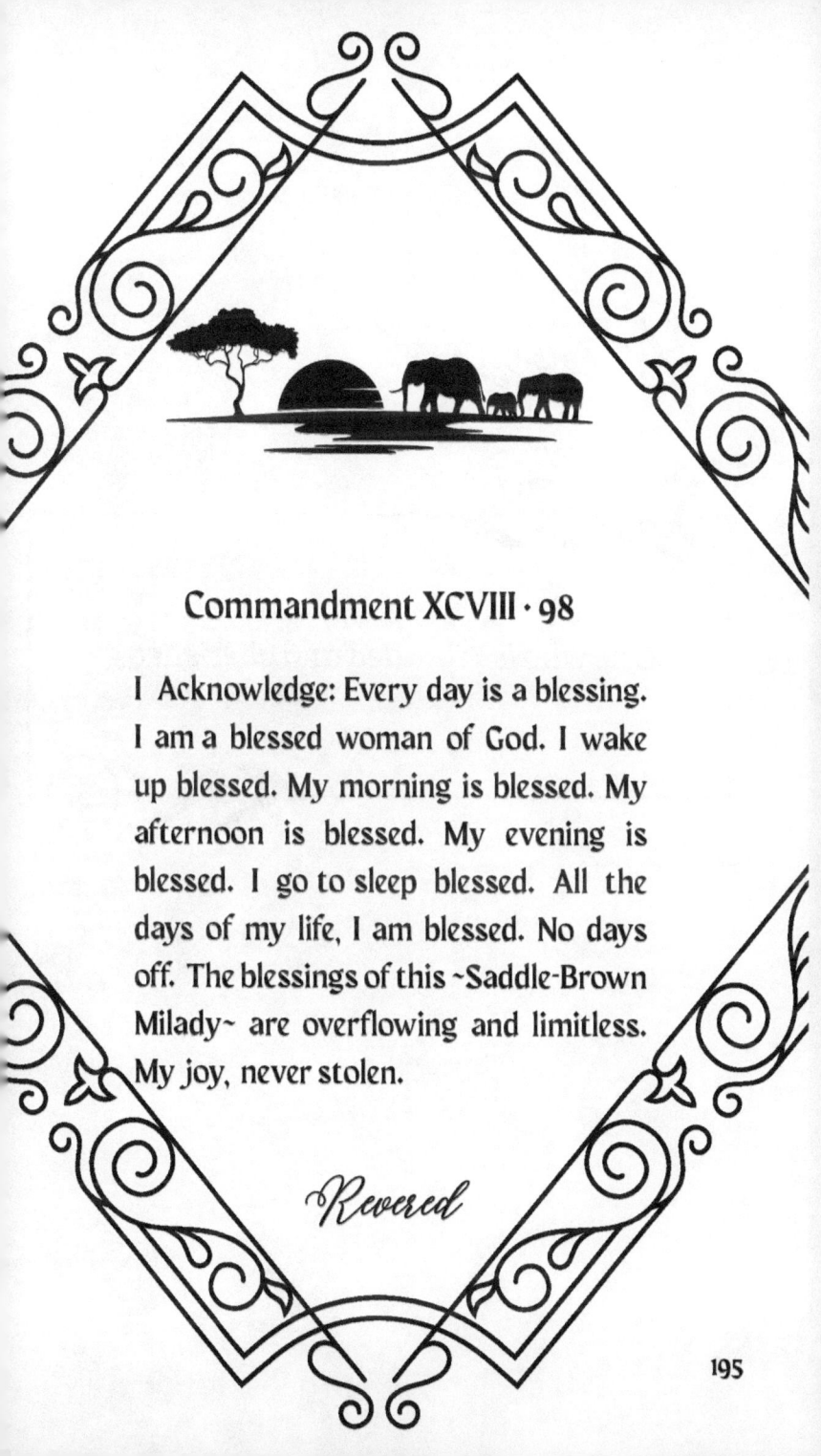

Commandment XCVIII · 98

I Acknowledge: Every day is a blessing. I am a blessed woman of God. I wake up blessed. My morning is blessed. My afternoon is blessed. My evening is blessed. I go to sleep blessed. All the days of my life, I am blessed. No days off. The blessings of this ~Saddle-Brown Milady~ are overflowing and limitless. My joy, never stolen.

Revered

Revered

One who is regarded and cherished.

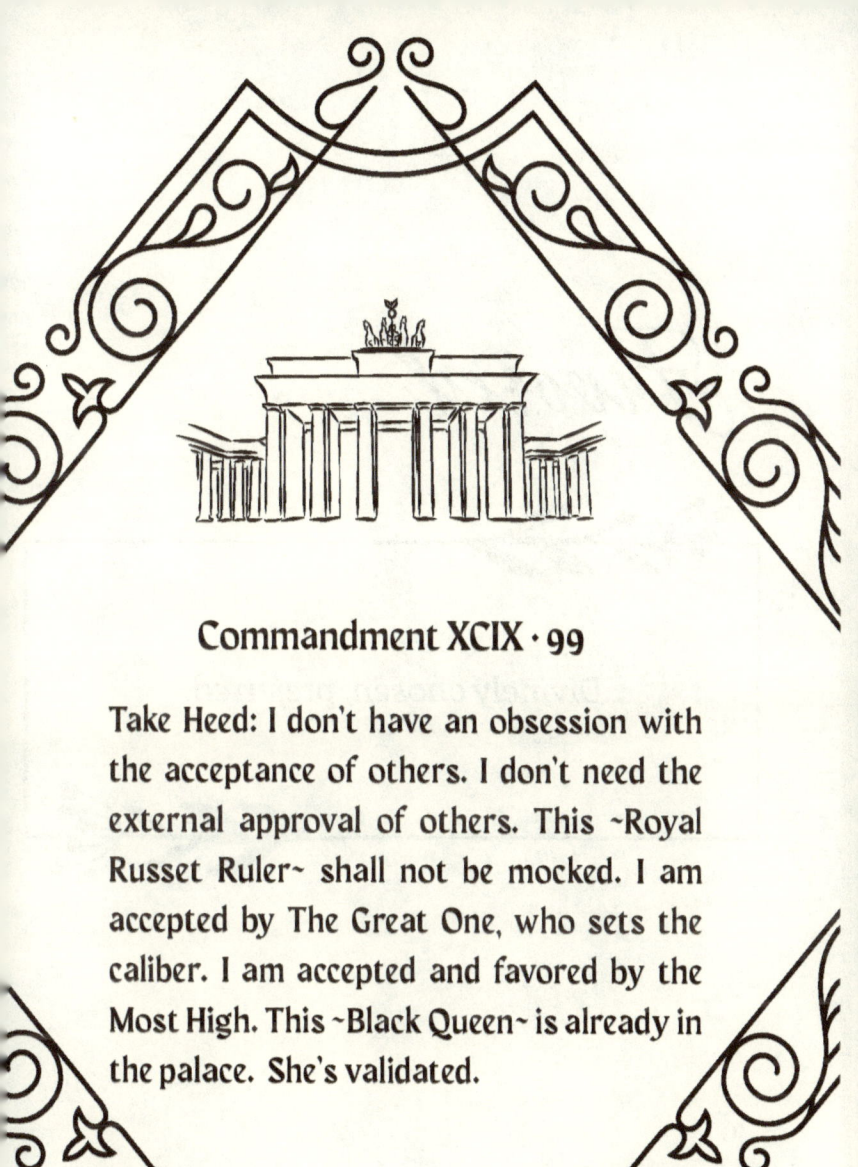

Commandment XCIX · 99

Take Heed: I don't have an obsession with the acceptance of others. I don't need the external approval of others. This ~Royal Russet Ruler~ shall not be mocked. I am accepted by The Great One, who sets the caliber. I am accepted and favored by the Most High. This ~Black Queen~ is already in the palace. She's validated.

Favored

Favored

Divinely chosen, preferred.

Commandment C · 100

Observe: I praise before the breakthrough. I am a Conqueress. I am the ~Obsidian-Oak Victoress~. I am the Frontrunner. I win every war. I remain undefeated. Victory is mine. Crowned in every season. My throne is permanent. Secured in my knowing. I am a ~Black Queen~.

Inspirer

Inspirer

A radiant force awakening greatness in others.

Letter to a Black Queen

Dear Black Queen,

Remember to love yourself. Honor yourself. Take care of yourself. Life sometimes is hard enough. It comes with challenges, but you were built to triumph over them. You were made to push through the hard stuff and still find the beauty in life.

God was so thoughtful when He created you. He knew exactly what He was doing. He designed you to love the dark hues and the very essence of your deep complexion; each shade woven with its own profound meaning. Your melanin sets you apart. It makes you powerful, it gives you presence. It makes you poised. You were called to do great things. You've been favored to carry them out.

Lift your head and adjust your tilted crown. Take charge and reign over your domain. You are a descendant of the Motherland. You come from legacy. Own who you are. Be what you were made of. You are royalty. It's your roots. It's your heritage. It's your bloodline. This is who you are.

.

Rise up Black Queen, your Queendom awaits.

Sincerely,

Livvy Liv, A Black Queen